Governing the World Economy

Titles in this series

Zygmunt Bauman, *Globalization: The Human Consequences*
Zygmunt Bauman, *Community: Seeking Safety
  in an Insecure World*
Norberto Bobbio, *Left and Right: The Significance of a
  Political Distinction*
Alex Callinicos, *Equality*
Diane Coyle, *Governing the World Economy*
Andrew Gamble, *Politics and Fate*
James Mayall, *World Politics: Progress and its Limits*
Ray Pahl, *On Friendship*

Governing the World Economy

DIANE COYLE

[signature: Diane Coyle]

Polity

First published in 2000 by Polity Press in association with Blackwell Publishers Ltd.

Editorial office: *Marketing and production*:
Polity Press   Blackwell Publishers Ltd
65 Bridge Street   108 Cowley Road
Cambridge CB2 1UR, UK   Oxford OX4 1JF, UK

Published in the USA by
Blackwell Publishers Inc.
350 Main Street
Malden, MA 02148, USA

A catalogue record for this book is available from the British Library.

Library of Congress Cataloging-in-Publication Data
Coyle, Diane.
   Governing the world economy / by Diane Coyle.
      p. cm.—(Themes for the 21st century)
   Includes bibliographical references and index.
   ISBN 0–7456–2363–8—ISBN 0–7456–2364–6 (pbk.)
   1. Free trade. 2. International finance. 3. Globalization. I. Title. II. Series.
HF1713.C695 2000
382′.71—dc21

                                                            00–034703

Typeset in 10.5 on 12 pt Plantin
by SetSystems, Saffron Walden, Essex
Printed in Great Britain by T. J. International, Padstow, Cornwall

This book is printed on acid-free paper.

Contents

Acknowledgements

I have drawn on the expertise of many researchers and of officials in international organisations, Treasuries and central banks in writing this book, and owe them a huge debt of gratitude. I would like to thank my colleagues at *The Independent*, particularly Matt Hoffman, Hamish McRae, Philip Thornton and Jeremy Warner, for their advice and support. Discussions with Ed Mayo, Andrew Simms and Raj Thamotheram were enormously helpful. I am also grateful to all the participants in a City Monetary Group seminar in May 1999 and a Foreign Policy Centre seminar in February 2000. As always, nothing would have been possible without Rory, Adam and Rufus. And of course responsibility for errors and omissions is entirely mine.

Introduction

It appeared to come completely out of the blue.

On the evening of Friday, 18 June 1999, a demonstration by around 4,000 people in the City of London, cheerfully billed as a 'carnival against capitalism', started to turn violent. A handful of protesters were arrested, some injured, and a few windows around central London were smashed. As well as the London International Financial Futures and Options Exchange and a couple of banks, a McDonald's – the people's restaurant if ever there was one – along with random premises such as the Royal Commonwealth Society, was damaged.

The following day the German city of Cologne saw a far bigger, peaceful demonstration against international capitalism. Campaigners against third world debt, many from church coalitions, formed a human chain around the hall where the annual G8 summit of the seven leading industrial countries – the US, Japan, Germany, France, Italy, the UK and Canada – and Russia was being held. The summit did result in an agreement to reduce the debt payments of about forty very poor countries, a financial package worth around $70bn. Nevertheless, campaigners denounced it as inadequate, demanding the complete forgiveness of the $300bn or so very poor countries owe to the International

Monetary Fund, World Bank and other official international organisations.

The next target for street protest was the World Trade
Organisation. Its annual meeting in Seattle at the beginning of December 1999 was a landmark for campaigners.
Their protests successfully called into question the WTO's
agenda, and beyond it the shape of the global economy.
This body, responsible for guaranteeing and extending the
freedom to trade across national boundaries, had spent
months in 1999 deadlocked over its future: would it be
run by Mike Moore, a US-backed New Zealander, or
Supachai Panitchpakdi, a Thai favoured by many developing countries? Members never did make up their minds,
opting to give the two candidates half a term of office
each.

Astonishingly for such an arcane and frankly dull organisation, its first annual meeting in Geneva in November
1998 had drawn the same kind of mass anti-finance, anti-
globalisation demonstrations, although these had pro-
ceeded peacefully. After mishandling by police turned the
marches in Seattle between 30 November and 1 December 1999 into a full-scale riot seen around the world, the
protest is clearly becoming an annual event in the calendar
of many non-governmental organisations.

Such voices of protest against international capitalism,
or globalisation, have had plenty of fresh ammunition and
some top-notch support in recent times. The financial
crisis that started with the devaluation of the Thai currency in July 1997, and spread to other South East Asian
countries that autumn, had moved on to Russia in August
1998. Having failed to satisfy the terms of its latest
agreement with the International Monetary Fund – which
was making the biggest loans in its history to the country
– Russia devalued and also defaulted on payments on its
Soviet-era international debts.

The knock-on effects on other types of international lending had consequences that were nearly catastrophic for the entire western banking system. Some hedge funds – a general term for offshore, unregulated investment funds that engage in complex transactions in a huge range of financial markets – had bet wrong on how bond markets would respond. Long Term Capital Management, a hedge fund run by a famous Wall Street trader and two Nobel Prize-winners in economics, nearly went bankrupt. Unfortunately, some of the biggest US, British and German banks had lent it large sums of money to invest on their behalf without enough security and without knowing much about what it was doing. It was not too hard for the US central bank, the Federal Reserve Board, to persuade the banks to rescue LTCM. Its bankruptcy could have brought some of them down. The ripple through the rest of the banking system would have been the biggest financial catastrophe since the Great Depression.

The Fed also cut interest rates in the US three times in rapid succession to lubricate the fragile banking system. It was probably essential at the time, but it stored up trouble for the future by inflating the Wall Street stockmarket bubble even further. That has not yet burst as I write (July 2000), although it will. Even putting a potential crash in share prices out of their minds, there is no doubt that the most senior figures in the world of international finance were extremely worried men in the autumn of 1998. At the G7 summit and annual IMF meeting in Washington in October there was an air of near-panic unprecedented in my experience of such events. The world leaders and finance ministers commissioned expert papers and scurried to make high-profile statements about the need to reform the 'international financial architecture'.

As I write, the gloomiest predictions of global slump and financial collapse have not come true. The South East Asian economies where it all started in 1997 are clearly recovering. The cost has been genuine hardship in countries where there is no welfare safety net, but even so the worst crisis in half a century appears to have resulted in just two years' lost output, making it a common-or-garden recession rather than a full-blown depression. And many western economies have benefited from improved purchasing power and lower world prices for goods as much as they have lost through shrinking export markets. However, it could yet all go badly wrong. Japan is still in a true slump. A Wall Street crash could derail tentative global economic recovery. So far the share price bubble appears to have nothing worse than a slow puncture, but it could easily turn into a far more alarming decline. China might devalue its currency to alleviate slow growth, triggering another leg of the financial crisis. It is also true that the 1997–8 crisis was another chapter in the story begun in 1994–5 with the Mexican crisis. This tale of instability is not over yet.

The events in Seattle outside and inside the meeting of ministers from 134 WTO member countries have taken the story a stage further. The rolling anti-capitalism protests occur now at every prominent official international meeting. There were further demonstrations in Washington outside the headquarters of the International Monetary Fund in April 2000, where officials and ministers had to leave their hotels literally at the crack of dawn to avoid the whiff of tear gas and blocked roads. The continuing series of protest events underlines the self-advertisement on one of the placards prominent in the Washington demonstration: 'World campaign against globalization.' For the first time a serious public debate about globalisation and liberalisation is taking place. This had been entirely absent for some fifteen years up to the mid-1990s. For example, the predecessor of the WTO, the General Agreement on Tariffs and Trade, could not drum up any interest in the culmination of the previous round of world trade talks which ended in 1994. The development of public debate must be healthy. There is a clear political warning in recent outbursts against global capitalism and the project of economic integration of free markets, characterised by many as the 'One World' project.

There is a definite sense in public debate that the global economy is being run for the benefit of the few at the expense of the many. This perception has helped make debt relief such a popular cause. It has helped fuel suspicion of the multinational corporations that want to export genetically modified foods. Environmental groups, churches, aid agencies, New Age travellers and trade unions, amongst others, have coalesced into an informal (although increasingly Internet-organised) coalition in opposition to the existing structures of the global economic system.

Yet it is one thing to argue that the international financial system needs improvement, another to write it off as rotten beyond repair without having a replacement in mind. Many of those who oppose the IMF or WTO or G7 oppose them as symbols, without a credible alternative political agenda. There is a pure romanticism in much of the protest, a desire to turn the clock back and return to a simpler time. While the concerns of this tradition are honourable – concern for the dignity and autonomy of different peoples, suspicion of unaccountable technocrats and powerful financial interests – I will argue they are more likely to harm than help the poor and dispossessed.

The only way to empower the poor is for them to become less poor. Developing countries need to grow. While there is still heated debate amongst economists

about what causes or boosts economic growth, it is clear
that it involves a mainly market-based economy which
protects property rights, provides a stable macroeconomic
framework and permits the freedom to exchange, including across international borders. Beyond this, it is not
clear what boosts growth – what kind of labour market
institutions, what tax system, what international financial
framework. Ideology does not have the answers; pragma-
tism does. The alternative opposition, anti-market model
is as unlikely as the Thatcherite or Reaganite neo-liberal
model to be right for all countries. Critics of the market-
based status quo, however, have no adequate response to
the observation that it has actually delivered massive
improvements in living standards to countries that
adopted its minimum requirements. The world financial
crisis does not negate the fact that average living standards
in Korea and Taiwan now match those in Greece and
Portugal within a generation of their first engagement in
the world market economy.

Many in the 'world opposition' are also just as imperi-
alist in their prescriptions as the IMF. There is little
understanding that imposing a set of environmental standards on developing countries through trade rules, for
example, would be exactly parallel to imposing the 'Multilateral Agreement on Investment' (MAI), a proposed
treaty much hated by environmentalists and others
because it was seen as a charter for multinational profits.
Both types of proposal are designed for the benefit of
certain interests in developed countries, and might or
might not help developing economies, depending on their
details.

Detail matters. It is important, for example, in trying to
decide whether capital controls could usefully slow or
prevent financial market crises. The answer is that it
depends on exactly what kinds of controls and when they

are introduced. Similarly, any assessment of the IMF's track record must rely on details of specific programmes, for its macroeconomic medicine tends to help particular groups in particular countries at the expense of others – but not always in the obvious way. IMF austerity programmes imposed on high-spending governments in high-inflation developing countries have often helped the very poor at the expense of the privileged bureaucratic classes.

This might seem like nit-picking at a time of apparent systemic collapse. The pervading sense that globalisation has smashed at full pelt into a brick wall and Something Must Be Done has been reinforced by many eminent doers and thinkers. George Soros rushed out a book on the crisis of capitalism, comparing the process of globalisation to a wrecking ball destroying any country in its path.[1] The following year, Paul Krugman, Professor of Economics at the Massachusetts Institute of Technology, published *The Return of Depression Economics*, urging the abandonment of IMF-style financial orthodoxy at a time when a third of the world's nations were in recession.[2] There have been countless other much less well-informed and far more breathless books in the same vein. Anybody protesting outside an international financial gathering can stuff their back-pack with reading matter that will validate their indignation.

It is easy to spot parallels between the globalisation of today, triggered by technological and political change, and the episode of globalisation a century ago. But it is not an entirely comfortable parallel. After all, while that earlier episode did bring huge increases in prosperity, it involved massive political turmoil as societies struggled to keep pace with economic change. Alarmingly, there is already ample evidence that the fruits of today's changes are benefiting the privileged alone. According to UN figures, in 1960 the fifth of the world's population in the richest countries had thirty times the income of the poorest fifth. The ratio is now seventy-four times. Income inequality is widening between countries and within countries, and even within separate professions. The net worth of the world's two hundred richest people increased from $440bn to $1 trillion in just four years from 1994 to 1998. By then, there were nearly two billion humans living on less than $1 a day. With this in mind, it is easy to understand what motivates the new opposition movement.

This is a book about global political economy written in a different spirit, however. It is a defence of globalisation and of free markets – a defence likely to appear contrary or provocative to its intended audience but one needed ḥeċause the intellectual tide has turned so violently against the earlier neo-liberal caricature of free-market economics. The backlash is going too far. This is an attempt at constructive engagement, sympathising with the spirit of backlash while trying to identify which of its criticisms are valid and which not.

1

Frankenstein Finance

One of the sub-genres of popular literature to emerge in the past two decades has been the financial gothic. Sometimes presented as outright fiction, more often as factual – although with a heavy dose of fantasy – these books portray a bizarre world few of us have ever experienced. It is the world of the big investment banks, or rather the sub-sections of these banks where overpaid, overgrown schoolboys trade in various financial instruments. Just a few dozen trading floors in New York and London stand at the hub of the global financial markets. With their disturbing or incomprehensible conventions and brutal culture, which we see in the chink of light shed by books written by former employees, these bond and derivatives traders seem to threaten the stability of the world economy. And, like Frankenstein's monster, we created them ourselves.

Forget the rationale for financial markets, their efficiency at raising funds for investment, the higher returns they can deliver investors, or any such theoretical advantage. The traders' aim is to make as much money as possible in as short a time as possible and hang the consequences. That's money for themselves, not the bank that employs them. Their bonus, often greater by far than their salary, depends on their group's profit in one year.

Next year they can always get another job. The hours are long, the carousing hard and anybody not part of the group is the enemy. The extreme conditions make for a macho environment where customers matter only because they are the prey.

One recent contribution to the financial gothic literature describes the development of investment by US and European pension and insurance funds in emerging markets during the early 1990s as the result of a marketing campaign by creative investment bankers.[1] They devised investments acceptable to pension fund trustees by disguising their inherent riskiness and boosting the apparent investment return with clever derivatives. The purpose was generating commission, and a successful deal was described as 'ripping people's faces off'. The author modestly claims much of the credit for the Mexican financial crisis in 1994–5 thanks to his devising a derivative that allowed the country's banks to borrow in US dollars and allowed US investors to put money in high-return Mexican investments disguised as safe, American dollar ones.

Derivatives are synthetic financial investments created by packaging characteristics of underlying assets such as shares or government bonds. They are 'derived', in other words. If investing in shares is gambling, then investing in derivatives is a bet on a bet. They can switch the interest paid on one type of asset in one currency for another, changing the time-horizon and the degree of risk involved in the investment. Often derivatives can reduce risk or raise expected investment returns. Sometimes they do the opposite. It is difficult for anybody who is not an expert to tell which is which. It is evident from a number of high-profile derivatives scandals, such as the bankruptcy of Orange County, California, or big losses made by companies like Procter & Gamble and Metallgesellschaft, that some supposed experts cannot tell either.

There have, however, been many, many more success-ful derivatives transactions than disasters. They are used profitably every day by all investment managers and cor-porate treasuries. There is no cast-iron estimate of the size of the derivatives transactions outstanding, although it exceeds $70 trillion or equivalent to about eight times the annual GDP of the United States or the capitalisation of the US stockmarket. The scale of the disasters is tiny by comparison with this total. But the financial gothic has set the tone for our understanding of these markets. It is the monsters of the trading floors who run the markets and, through them, our lives. They are apparently fuelled by junk food, black coffee and cocaine, their lethal weapons their banks of mysterious screens of figures and charts. Even if the growing sell-and-tell literature produced by former traders exaggerates the scene, however, it is cer-tainly true that stamina, sheer nerve and a facility for mental arithmetic matter more than brainpower and cool-headed analysis in the markets. The live trading pits of the big derivatives exchanges like the Chicago Board of Trade or the Mercantile Exchange are fading into history but they will remain unforgettable for anybody who has visited them. The second the opening bell rang, the noise as traders in bright, tacky jackets began to gesticulate from their cramped positions elbow-to-elbow around the pits struck the listener as a physical crump of sound that made the floor vibrate. Never mind mental arithmetic, brawn alone was the chief characteristic here. These potential rugby prop forwards were the mainstay of the derivatives markets.

This narrative has informed reactions to the hedge fund crisis in the summer of 1998. Ever since George Soros, one of the earliest and most prominent hedge fund man-agers, forced the UK out of the European Exchange Rate Mechanism in September 1992 by speculating against sterling in the currency markets, these funds have been popular scapegoats in any financial market turmoil. Mahathir bin Mohamad, Malaysia's prime minister, stridently blamed Soros and other speculators for the Asian crisis in 1997. A careful study by the IMF found hedge funds had played little role in events that year – most of them had got out of South East Asia much earlier. Even so, despite evidence that much of the capital flight involves domestic rather than foreign investors bailing out, few observers are willing to exonerate them. Many leading figures in Hong Kong firmly believe hedge funds co-operated to attack the Hong Kong dollar's peg to the US dollar in 1998. This attack was unsuccessful because the authorities unexpectedly intervened in the stockmarket, buying up shares to stabilise the local markets – a drastic step for such a free-market administration. Hong Kong officials have shared this opinion widely.

Never popular even in the tame financial crises of the 1960s when it was Zurich financiers who famously got the blame, speculators are feared even more now they have so much more power. How have they gained this extra power? The answer is threefold. It lies in politics, technology and economics. The political aspect is the deregulation of financial markets that began in the 1970s but gathered pace the following decade. The US and UK took the lead with moves to liberalise capital flows in and out of each country that helped cement the advantage of New York and London as financial centres – more capital will flow into places it can easily leave. The 'Big Bang' deregulation of the City of London in 1986 played a key part in the subsequent stranglehold London gained in currency markets. Financial deregulation was also certainly a prominent aspect of the Thatcher–Reagan philosophy, although one whose consequences the two governments had not necessarily thought through to their logical conclusions.

According to a former minister in the Thatcher government, the thought process did not amount to a lot more than: 'Well, why not remove these old restrictions?'

This free-market political gloss on the decision was in a way just catching up with the reality that the controls on flows of money across borders, so fundamental to the Bretton Woods system of fixed exchange rates, were already crumbling. Even before 1973, when the fixed parities were first abandoned, big companies and investors were able to evade the restrictions when they really wanted to – if the controls had really been watertight, there could not have been a sterling crisis six years earlier.

Barry Eichengreen, in his history of the global monetary system, argues that capital controls were only effective during the immediate post-war years when governments intervened extensively in all aspects of their economies. 'Controls held back the flood because they were not just one rock in a swiftly flowing stream. They were part of a series of levees and locks with which the raging rapids were tamed.'[2] Even by the 1960s, when war-time economic planning had vanished, capital controls could not work. The extent to which they could not work became more apparent as world trade and direct foreign investment grew. It became increasingly difficult to tell which of the increasing number of foreign currency transactions were genuinely required by trade or multinational production, and which were speculative. The foreign exchange restrictions were increasingly breached in practice.

The gradual political liberalisation has been accompanied by technological changes that made it much easier and cheaper to shift money around. Although many of the necessary advances in computer and telecommunications technologies had been made by the early 1970s, this, too, was a gradual process that has only reached its full potential in the past fifteen or twenty years with the changing management and ownership of banks. It is only recently that the banks operating in London and New York have merged and moved into buildings with huge trading floors, allowing them to exploit fully the technological economies of scale. But steadily as more and more banks and brokers in more financial centres have switched over from physical to electronic trading, and as telecoms costs have declined, the speed and scale of potential financial flows have soared.

However, more significant than either of these in the expansion of the global markets has been the growth in demand for what the markets do – namely raising funds for borrowers. And the big borrowers are governments. Governments in the leading industrial countries all turned to the financial markets. It started on a large scale with the US in the Vietnam War, but all governments borrowed to finance growing deficits during the 1970s. This took place first behind a veil of Keynesian economic orthodoxy – government borrowing was deemed to be acceptable if it was used for domestic demand management – and then out of habit. The total gap between G7 governments' revenues and expenditures, or, in other words, the amount governments did not care to ask their taxpayers to finance, grew from around zero during the 1950s and 1960s to around 5 per cent of national income by the end of the 1970s – the highest and most sustained it had ever been in peace-time.

The creation of very big government bond markets was a precondition for the growth of other financial markets. International investors often had to be attracted to buy bonds. The size and liquidity of government bond markets made it easier for markets in other financial instruments to develop in the same centres. The necessary habits and expertise were created. And the existence of emerged markets ultimately made sense of the notion of emerging markets, whereby governments in other parts of the world could borrow money in the financial markets too. What used to be called third world debt, owed to the IMF and World Bank, was transmogrified into emerging market debt owed by similar countries to private investors. This is the sense in which the financial markets are really monsters of our own creation.

Recent financial crises

There is nothing new about crisis in financial markets. Speculative bubbles are at least as old as the tulip mania in 1630s Holland and the South Sea Bubble, which burst spectacularly in 1720. However, there is a widespread feeling that the crises are both more frequent and more severe than in the past. This is somewhat misleading, although recent financial turmoil is different in character.

The Bretton Woods era (1946–73) specialised in currency crises. Governments were for the most part unwilling to concede they needed to devalue their exchange rates to adjust for higher domestic inflation, for an exchange rate pegged against other currencies needs to decline when the domestic purchasing power of the 'pound in your pocket' has already been devalued. Speculation against troubled currencies would mount as their governments spent reserves financing balance of payments deficits. Devaluations became more and more frequent in the late 1960s. The eventual collapse of the fixed exchange rate system was superseded by the oil price shocks in the 1970s. These, in turn, generated the generalised financial and economic crises in countries such as the UK and Italy in the late 1970s, with their yawning government deficits, balance of payments deficits, falling exchange rates and soaring domestic interest rates.

The subsequent decade saw isolated episodes of financial volatility in the industrial countries – for example, when the new Socialist government in France tried a public spending spree in 1981 the franc fell sharply as capital deserted the country. The episode was widely interpreted as an ideologically motivated attack by the financial markets on a Socialist government. While this is to attribute too great a coherence to the markets, it is true that most participants adhere firmly to the conventional economic orthodoxy of the day.

The attack on the French franc aside, the 1980s were dominated by the third world debt crisis, notably in Latin America. The new wealth of the oil-producing countries had been 'recycled' by western banks in loans to developing countries in the second half of the previous decade. With loans extended on an unsustainable scale and incautious terms to countries in turn running unsustainable macroeconomic policies, it was a crisis waiting to happen, and one with devastating economic and social consequences in the affected nations. Western banks were prepared to overlook bad policies initially in the rush for business but, predictably, turned against them when conditions changed for the worse. The burden of debt interest payments and the financial penalties of renegotiating the loans overshadowed Latin American growth for years. There was, however, one sense in which it was an easier crisis to resolve than the more recent ones. Most of the loans had been made by a relatively small number of big US and European banks, so it was ultimately easier for the US authorities to persuade or bully the bankers into negotiating new terms with the debtor countries.

The 1990s saw one episode of financial upheaval after another. The first, in 1992 and 1993, brought speculation against the weakest currencies in Europe's Exchange Rate Mechanism, a system of fixed but adjustable exchange rates. Speculators, including, as we have seen, George Soros, forced the pound to leave despite an estimated 10bn spent on its defence by the Bank of England. The lira left temporarily, the French franc also came under pressure, and the margins by which member currencies were allowed to vary had to be permanently widened.

No sooner had the European markets quietened than the emerging market investment boom laid the foundations for the most recent episodes. As well as big loans from big banks, the new pattern was for masses of investment and pension funds to pile individual investors' savings directly into developing countries' stockmarkets. And the amounts invested in this way soared. Total net private investment in the developing countries by corporations, banks and investors from the rich OECD countries climbed from $100bn in 1990 to a record $214bn in 1996. Of this, $114bn took the form of direct foreign investment by companies in factories, with the rest 'portfolio' investment in the local financial and property markets, or bank loans.

The first scare came in December 1994 when Mexico devalued the peso, which had been fixed in value against the dollar. The country had been booming, and the boom sucked in imports creating a trade deficit. To keep the currency stable, the Mexican central bank had been forced to use its foreign exchange reserves to buy pesos. In such circumstances something eventually has to give, and the Mexican government – as most do in such circumstances – opted for devaluation as the easiest way out. It was a big miscalculation. Mexican banks had such large debts in US dollars that a cheaper Mexican currency meant they might be unable to meet the interest payments on their foreign loans. Sensible overseas lenders demanded immediate repayment. Other foreign investors, who had seen their investment returns slashed in terms of their own currencies, rushed to pull their money out of the country before things got any worse. So did Mexican investors. There was a stampede for the exit.

The US Treasury in the shape of Lawrence Summers, then Deputy Treasury Secretary, put together a $50bn emergency loan to Mexico and the IMF dictated tough policies to the Mexican government, despite a rebellion in the Chiapas region. The country's financial markets had stabilised by mid-1995 – a swift recovery. The economy took a year longer to start pulling out of recession. But even that can be seen as a rapid bounce back from what was then the biggest-ever international financial rescue. The crisis also prompted a good deal of soul-searching at the IMF. Why had they not seen it coming? In fact they had, up to a point, as had many individual private sector economists, but had kept private the warnings they gave about the errors and inadequacies of policy in their regular discussions with the Mexican government. The Fund made absolutely no public expression of concern. The herd in the financial markets had therefore completely ignored the classic warning symptoms of an overheating economy – the current account deficit, the dwindling reserves – in an equally classic example of mania followed by panic.

The IMF response was to make a huge public display of the importance of 'surveillance' by private investors of emerging market countries. For instance, with much fanfare it started a programme to publish on the Internet regular and timely statistics on its member economies. The onus was on the individual countries to provide information to the highest standard they could manage, and investors were to learn to differentiate between countries according to the quality of the information they could or would provide.

Improved surveillance unfortunately proved inadequate two years later. In a repeat of the Mexico episode, in July

1997 the Thai baht was forced to devalue from its previously pegged level. The central bank had used up its reserves, although disguising the true situation through 'forward' deals in the foreign exchange markets giving it more reserves now at the price of fewer later. The panic sent the Bangkok stockmarket diving and also caused a collapse in property prices in the formerly booming real estate business. Once again, some investors and analysts had warned about Thailand's financial vulnerability months before the crisis occurred, but their caution had not been enough to defuse the investment mania.

Unfortunately, this crisis was not a simple repetition of the Mexican one. For it spread to neighbouring countries in South East Asia, some in similar circumstances, others that were fundamentally much healthier. Some – notably Taiwan and Singapore – escaped completely, while others – such as China and Hong Kong – weathered the upheavals, though with some difficulty. Nevertheless, the contagion spread, first to Malaysia and Indonesia, then on to South Korea by the winter. Despite its utterly cautious and orthodox macroeconomic policies, and its recent admission to the OECD, foreign and local investors started to pull money out of South Korea. They did so on such a scale that the ability of South Korean banks and companies to meet their debts came into question, making the panic self-fulfilling. The US Treasury and IMF had to ride to the rescue once again with a package of loans worth $71bn to the Asian Tigers. The Fund imposed tough economic programmes. Its then managing director, Michel Camdessus, was foolish enough to be photographed standing over Indonesia's President Suharto as he signed the IMF Letter of Intent – Washington imperialism personified.

The IMF came under severe criticism for sticking to its conventional economic orthodoxies in South East Asia.

While the measures might have been appropriate for Thailand, it was hard to see why a good pupil like South Korea should be forced to take the same medicine. The IMF's defence was, essentially, that, despite its good record, South Korea, too, had to reassure foreign investors so their funds would return.

Moreover, the conventional wisdom explaining the contagion in Asia – where Japan was separately stuck in severe recession – blamed 'crony capitalism'. Even where governments had been running good macroeconomic policies, it was argued, corruption, nepotism and the general failure to impose the full disciplines of a market economy explained why investors carried on running away once the dash for the exits had been triggered.

Malaysia rebelled against western triumphalism. Prime Minister Mahathir stormed into the IMF's annual meeting in Hong Kong in September 1997 denouncing George Soros and 'Jewish' speculators, and any other culprits. He subsequently imposed capital controls on movements of money into and out of Malaysia, and trumped up charges against Anwar Ibrahim, his more conventional finance minister. President Suharto's government fell in Indonesia, resulting in democratic elections. The political situation in the strife-ridden country remained uncertain, with savage violence erupting in some parts of the archipelago.

The economies and markets of all four countries – Thailand, Malaysia, Indonesia and South Korea – had stabilised after the first year, however. All except Indonesia were staging an impressive recovery by mid-1999, though at higher levels of unemployment and with severe social dislocations. Some, like South Korea, had accomplished this by following IMF advice to the letter. Malaysia managed a degree of recovery while defying Washington wisdom, imposing capital controls which – as even the Fund eventually conceded – had given the economy a valuable breathing space.

But they were not the last victims of the turmoil. August 1998 brought, for very different reasons, the Russian crisis. Russia devalued the rouble and defaulted on part of its international debts using the global crisis as cover for a domestic political failure to take tough decisions. The IMF had been pouring money into Russia, but a succession of governments had failed to meet the attached conditions. Indeed, business oligarchs, rather than the politicians meeting Fund officials, were taking key decisions. The scale of the Russian crisis was amplified by the accident of LTCM's investment losses, and the potential consequences for the western banking system. Global financial meltdown appeared imminent. Investors everywhere piled out of any market that appeared at risk in favour of the safety of US Treasury bonds. Even Wall Street took a bit of a tumble.

The full behind-the-scenes story of discussions in the centres of power in the US, the massive, pillared Treasury Department building, the equally imposing Federal Reserve Board down the road in Washington, and its barrack-like New York satellite, has not yet been told. Yet the frenzy of meetings and the rescue of Long Term Capital succeeded in calming world financial markets. Alan Greenspan, chairman of the US Federal Reserve Board, cut interest rates three times in succession in September and October 1998 just to make sure.

In December 1998 Brazil fell victim to the same kind of devaluation crisis, despite a supposedly pre-emptive emergency loan package negotiated two months earlier. But by this time the steam had gone out of the panic. The replacement of the central bank governor by a Brazilian fund manager working with George Soros marked the end of the episode, and Brazil recovered almost astonishingly quickly. The only question is how long it will be until the next panic somewhere in the world's financial markets, with Wall Street itself looking the likeliest candidate at the time of writing.

The lessons

There have been essentially two reactions to the rolling crisis that started in mid-1997: blame the governments and blame the markets. The first camp points to the institutional weaknesses in countries into which investors had been so enthusiastically herding – the crony capitalism or nomenklatura capitalism argument – and says essentially that developing countries need to try to become more like democratic, developed countries in their politics and institutions if they are to avoid economic and financial crises. This bears a philosophical relationship to the 'end of history' school, which saw in the collapse of communism in 1989 the ultimate vindication of liberal democracy and market capitalism.[3] The second blames the tidal washes of global capital for inherent instability and favours direct restrictions such as capital controls or a tax on 'speculative' investment, or re-regulation of the markets.

Before assessing each of these extremes in turn, it is worth trying to set the scene with a few wider conclusions from the latest two-year episode of instability. First, Robert Skidelsky has pointed out that the decades just before and after the Second World War were characterised by financial crisis in the developed economies, whereas the most recent crises, like those in the nineteenth and the early twentieth century, have mainly affected the developing 'periphery'.[4] True, some, like the US Savings and Loans crisis in the early 1980s or that affecting Swedish banks in the 1990s, have occurred in the core. And it was the threatened spread of financial instability from periphery to core that prompted the structure of capital controls devised at Bretton Woods, as these could prevent contagion and allow governments to determine national income levels. However, even since their removal, crisis has remained a peripheral phenomenon. Although some western investors lost money in 1997 and 1998, the turmoil carefully sidestepped the OECD economies, apart from South Korea. That sense of panic in August 1998 stemmed from the fear that perhaps, at last, crisis was moving to the core, but it was averted by the skin of Alan Greenspan's teeth when the Federal Reserve chairman cut US interest rates rapidly to stabilise the financial system.

Secondly, the entire episode demonstrates the extent to which global markets are closely linked. Thailand's problems started when the US Federal Reserve Board raised American interest rates in February 1997 in order to touch the brakes of the domestic economy and let off some of the steam building up on Wall Street. The dollar appreciated, and so, thanks to its peg to the US currency, did the Thai baht. That worsened Thailand's current account deficit, setting off the subsequent chain of events. A global economy with such a dominant centre has pretty stark implications for other countries' monetary and exchange rate policies. In the absence of restrictions on capital flows, there is essentially a choice between using interest rates for domestic economic management or sacrificing interest rate policy to achieve a fixed exchange rate peg. The 1990s crises demonstrated that in the end the peg will break – no government can raise interest rates high enough to defend a given exchange rate throughout an investor panic.

This moral has been drawn in Washington and elsewhere. The IMF will in future discourage developing countries from adopting a potentially breakable exchange rate link to the dollar. Any which want currency stability will essentially have to adopt the US dollar. Some, like Argentina, have been discussing actively whether or not to go ahead with 'dollarisation' whereby the Fed would essentially run Argentina's interest rate policy. The country already has a currency board, an arrangement where the authorities hold big enough reserves of US dollars to back the entire supply of domestic currency. The motivation for this is to give such a firm guarantee that the peso will not be devalued that the fear never arises in the minds of investors, so there is no danger of a speculative run on the currency ahead of an anticipated devaluation. But a currency board poses an obvious question: if the government already accepts the restrictions imposed by the need for the domestic currency to be as good as the US currency, why not just use dollars and scrap the peso? Monetary policy is already restricted by the demands of the currency board. Why not eliminate the remaining risk of devaluation entirely? The debate between the Argentine and US authorities has been entirely serious, and dollarisation could still go ahead.

Of course, a similar dilemma applies to higher-income countries. One of the rationales underlying European Monetary Union was the desire to escape from its horns, to eliminate exchange rate crises within the EU even at the price of applying a common interest rate to all members. The near-breakup of the Exchange Rate Mechanism in the early 1990s spurred the creation of the single currency. The alternatives would have been the effective 'deutschmark-isation' of other EU currencies or the danger of repeat crises.

The basic point is that in a world of large and free-flowing capital movements, governments have limited policy options. In the end, you can blame the capital markets for setting the limits, or you can blame the governments for refusing to recognise them. But there is no way out of this dilemma.

Blame the governments

One of the few recent books to praise globalisation, almost without reservation, is *The Lexus and the Olive Tree* by Thomas Friedman, a writer on the *New York Times*. It is an extremely irritating book with a breathtaking conclusion: 'If you are not American . . . I suggest you learn,' Mr Friedman advises the rest of the planet.[5] (He was also the author of the patriotic observation that no two countries with a McDonald's restaurant had ever gone to war with each other, which was true only until Nato planes bombed Belgrade.) In a nutshell, this American economic imperialism is nevertheless the conclusion of many far less irksome authors. They deem the crisis to have demonstrated that so-called 'Asian values' of consensus, stable social relations, respect for authority, and so on, acclaimed by some theorists as the foundation of the economic success of the Tiger economies, are actually inferior to old-fashioned Anglo-Saxon values like competition and dissent.

Martin Feldstein, formerly an economic adviser to the Reagan White House, has noted that the recent crisis was an excuse for western policy-makers to force South Korea, which had just joined the rich nations' club of the OECD, to reshape itself in something more like the US image:

Although many of the structural reforms the IMF included in its early-December [1998] program for Korea would probably improve the long-term performance of the Korean economy, they are not needed for Korea to gain access to capital markets. They are also among the most politically-sensitive issues: labor market rules, regulations of corporate structure and governance, government–business relations and international trade. The specific policies the IMF insists must be changed are not so different from those in the major countries of Europe.[6]

As in all extreme views, there is a grain of truth at the heart of the American triumphalism. It is certainly true that the countries affected first and worst by the crisis were lacking in institutions of democratic accountability and were more corrupt than many developed nations. In addition, underdeveloped banking systems and rampant cronyism meant loans were without doubt being made unwisely – on the basis of personal connections rather than financial criteria.

Not sharing Feldstein's reservations, Friedman evidently sees the crisis as a cathartic force in Asia, driving out corrupt politicians. He writes: 'The herd [i.e. foreign investors] proved to be unlike any of their familiar domestic enemies. They could not arrest it, censor it, ban it, bribe it and often could not see it.' He goes on: 'It is not an accident that every country with a per capita income above $15,000 is a liberal democracy,' except Singapore – which will become one, he asserts.[7]

He forgets that the herd of investors has also been known to stampede over democratic governments, like those of France and the UK. He overlooks, too, the fact that consensus and traditional relations characterise some very successful economies like Germany. But beneath Friedman's exaggeration lurk a few relevant insights. Governments must indeed take some of the blame for the vulnerability of their countries to financial crisis. It is fair to blame bad policies for bad results. To do so is not *per se* an acceptance of free-market fundamentalism.

It is only during the decade or so of high Thatcherism

and Reaganism that free markets were ever understood as standing somehow outside social and political institutions. The radical neo-liberal agenda hijacked the idea of markets to mean a very specific set of institutions, namely the minimal, night-watchman state. However, economists dating back to Adam Smith, the founding father, have understood that markets work better in some contexts than others. Most recently the metaphor of 'social capital' has come into vogue as an explanation of why markets sometimes work and sometimes don't – Switzerland has a lot of it, the UK has plenty but perhaps less than it used to, and Russia has hardly any at all.

In short, markets operate in a context of law and custom, which determine how good the economic outcomes are. Amartya Sen has demonstrated that democracy and a free press can be a vital economic safeguard; democracies do not suffer catastrophic famines.[8] Although many countries have made great leaps in development without bothering with liberal democracy on the way, Dani Rodrik has shown that participatory political systems do help countries weather external economic shocks that cause conflict between different domestic constituencies.[9] The democratic process is what helps mediate economic conflict. So democracy makes a difference in bad times even if it does not in good times.

A strong rule of law which protects property rights vigorously will certainly help foster growth. So will laws to promote competition and limit monopoly, and the more rigorously enforced the better. A tradition of honouring deals – my word is my bond; the absence of violence in commercial relationships; meritocratic employment practices: all help markets work efficiently. The relevant institutional details are starting to be fleshed out by researchers. For instance, economic growth tends to be better wherever the Anglo-Saxon legal system applies, with its emphasis on contract, rather than the Napoleonic code, or where shareholders have the strongest financial rights, according to at least one piece of recent research carried out by the World Bank.[10] New OECD research also links growth to a vigorous stockmarket and strong share ownership culture.[11] These aspects of the American model do seem to produce a better economic performance.

On the other hand, aspects of American society are negatively linked to long-term economic performance. More equal societies tend to have a better growth record, and the US is very unequal. The links between education and growth are unclear in the extreme, but it would be hard to argue that the US education system is a model for Asian countries. Its health service is one of the most sophisticated in the world but as many as two-fifths of the population have no access to it. No developing country would build such a divisive system. America is also a violent society by most standards, which suggests that there are, to say the least, great lacunae in its social capital.

This is a debate with great resonance in Europe too. While Europeans would like to import some of the recent productivity growth and superb macroeconomic performance of the US, and many admire the transatlantic spirit of entrepreneurship and energy, few want to pay the price of inequality and social fracture. Whether the goods and bads have to go hand in hand, or whether instead it is possible to pick and choose aspects of American performance, is an urgent question.

Asian governments can certainly be blamed for getting some things wrong. In particular, they failed to adapt their financial systems to the rigours of large amounts of investment by foreigners used to operating under a completely different set of rules. The herd of investors thought Thailand and its fellow Tigers would learn to be just like

America in the dimensions that mattered, but the Thais did not realise that they had to. The IMF and World Bank have learned this lesson and now place great emphasis on financial reform taking place in step with financial liberalisation. Another important lesson is the absolute necessity of a social safety net in order to limit the real economic impact of financial crisis. Previously, social welfare had been seen as something of a luxury in development, something a country could postpone until it really had quite a lot of growth under its belt. There is nothing about globalisation that implies a minimal welfare state; on the contrary, the lesson of the 1990s is that it demands a strong social safety bedrock.

It is also true that the wave of crisis has revived the old-fashioned wisdom that governance matters, institutions matter, for markets to work well. The turmoil in Russia and the continuing stagnation of many Sub-Saharan African countries reinforce this conclusion. Indeed, good governance is what governments are for. Good microeconomic and social policies, rather than the sterility of the caricature Keynesian tax-and-spend approach, should be the aim of all governments – macro-stability and micro-dynamism is the ideal combination. Good government rather than big government. What the affected governments cannot be blamed for, however, is not being just like America. The US embodies just one variety of successful capitalism among many, and a version that has as many critics as admirers overseas. There is no one-size-fits-all set of market institutions for economic success.

Blame the markets

If blaming governments turns out to be a bit more subtle than some pundits proclaim, what about blaming markets?

Common sense seems to dictate that it cannot be sensible to allow bubbles of irrational enthusiasm in financial markets to build up only to burst with devastating real consequences like greater unemployment and hunger. History suggests that financial markets are innately prone to bubbles, and the only non-bubble periods, like the 1940s and 1950s, have occurred when there have not been free financial markets either.

It is impossible to envisage reconstruction of the kind of comprehensive capital controls that existed in the immediate post-war years. They could only operate in an economy with a degree of planning democracies have only tolerated in war-time and its aftermath. The next chapter looks in much greater depth at the international financial markets, but here I just want to consider their role in the Asia-plus crisis that started in 1997.

If there had not been so much western investment in the Tiger economies during the 1990s, the crisis would obviously have been different in its nature. But not very different, and not necessarily smaller. There is no question that a financial crash triggered the entire episode. Economists differ vigorously in the extent to which they believe there was a bubble in Asian financial markets – in other words, the degree to which share prices and property prices had raced ahead of some measure of their true or fundamental worth thanks to speculative mania and were therefore ripe for collapse. Some, like MIT's Paul Krugman, interpret events as a conventional banking panic, albeit taking place across borders, rather than anything particularly new and nasty about financial markets.[12] Others, like Harvard's Jeffrey Sachs, blame global financial market capitalism for inherent tendencies to excess and instability. He argued that there was a bubble burst in Thailand and Malaysia, that they suffered an avoidable and damaging bout of speculative excess.[13] Either way, the subsequent recessions in the affected countries originated in the financial markets.

The emerging markets boom amongst investors in the industrial countries also made us more aware as individuals of what was happening. We were aware that our pension fund or unit trust or mutual fund savings might well be at risk. Those who had invested in the Thai or Malaysian stockmarkets indeed lost money on paper and often in practice. In addition, many companies in the US and Europe which exported to Asia warned about the possible impact on their sales and ultimately on the number of people they could keep in jobs. However, exports to Asia form a very small proportion of total UK or US exports. Investment in factories and jobs in the developed countries by Asian Tigers was high-profile but also very small-scale. With hindsight, the extra danger to real economic growth brought about by the growth of the financial markets between 1987 and 1997 has turned out to be less than feared. Indeed it was minimal for the rich OECD countries. And the crisis countries themselves have in some ways recovered much faster than expected. Most turn out to have suffered a short recession that looks very sharp until you realise that the output loss was equivalent to two or three years' growth, like any recession. Slump it was not.

In other respects, the latest crisis has been a lot more similar to the Latin American debt crisis. This accords with the memory of central bank officials in the US and Europe who had to deal with both. If anything, western banks have been more effectively bailed out this time despite the greater size and complexity of the problem. But the economic and financial recovery in the affected countries has been faster too. It is, perhaps, still too early to be sure the crisis is over this time, but it looks increasingly as though the lavish official rescue loans organised

by the IMF have resolved financial problems more effectively than did the officially enforced renegotiation of
private sector bank loans in the early 1980s. While there
is a debate in policy circles about whether the IMF ought
to have bailed out the bankers so thoroughly, the fact that
it did do so seems to have helped stabilise the crisis very
rapidly.

There is a moral here, but it is not the obvious one that
bigger markets make for bigger crises. Meghnad Desai has
pointed out that the folk memory of the Great Depression
– often rescuscitated by people like J.K. Galbraith, whose
book on the subject[14] enjoys a surge in sales with every
episode of drama in the global financial markets – domi-
nates our assessment of the dangers. 'Much of our thinking of the likelihood of systemic instability is coloured by
this single and singular event,' Desai writes. 'We are in
some sense awaiting a Second Coming of the Great
Depression, but so far, no luck.'[15]

We are haunted by the financial gothic. This is not to
say markets cannot be unstable; they can. It is not to
argue that financial crashes do not have severe and unwel-
come real effects; they do. I simply want to point out that
much discussion of the financial markets lacks perspective.
It verges on the hysterical.

The true dark side of financial markets

In fact, there is astonishingly little mainstream attention
paid to the most serious drawback of vast, free capital
flows: the opportunities for crime they offer. Manuel
Castells is one honourable exception, with a detailed
analysis of the globalisation of organised crime in his
trilogy on the network society.[16] By its nature, evidence
on the scale of flows of tainted money is hard to come by,

but UN guesses indicate that it could be huge. Anecdotal evidence also points that way, and there are widespread reports on the growing co-operation between organised criminals from the traditional Mafia, triads and yakuza to the newer Russian gangs, Latin American drugs cartels, Turkish drugs runners, Nigerian fraudsters, Armenian traffickers, and so on.

In addition to the money laundering carried out to finance these vicious trades across national boundaries, the financial markets facilitate criminal corruption, making it easy for dictators and officials to salt away millions of dollars in secret bank accounts. Again, there are no reliable figures on the scale of this theft over the decades, but it has clearly been immense. Without it the sad history of many African nations might have been very different. And closer in on the spectrum of illegality, common-or-garden personal and corporate tax evasion, as well as legal avoidance, is also made far easier by the absence of restrictions on capital flows.

Governmental authorities are extremely concerned about criminal financial flows, although they tend not to give a high profile to the amount of effort they are forced to put into the battle, for obvious reasons. The Group of Eight summits (G7 plus Russia) always discuss the problem and set up the Financial Action Task Force at the OECD in Paris to co-ordinate national police and intelligence authorities in their efforts. The OECD also co-ordinates a drive against so-called 'unfair' tax competition, whereby multinational corporations force countries to reduce their tax burden through the implict or explicit threat of uprooting and taking the jobs elsewhere.

The biggest stumbling block in the battle against illegal financial flows is banking secrecy, although some headway has been made in persuading some countries to monitor the identity of their customers and report suspicious transactions. However, the cloak of banking secrecy is still widely used. It is not just notorious tax havens, nor the secretive banking centres of Zurich and Geneva, that hide behind it, but also banks in Austria, Germany and Luxembourg. (The Anglo-Saxon countries have the minimum banking secrecy.) Recent agreements by the EU and OECD to phase out this traditional secrecy might indicate it is now on the wane. It certainly ought to be. But while the most respectable investment funds in the US and Europe continue to operate from offshore tax havens to minimise the taxes they and their investors have to pay, and run their business through a network of subsidiary companies, it is going to be an uphill struggle for governments to combat the types of criminal activity where there really is a lot to hide.

And, of course, there is massive hypocrisy involved. For it is also national governments that cling to the secrecy laws in order to protect their powerful banking interests.

Any freedom can be undermined by criminal abuse. Licence has been the foe of liberty in many contexts, and it is just as true in the financial markets as in any other arena. Crime is therefore not in itself an argument for restrictions. However, the criminalisation of the global capital markets is indeed Frankenstein finance and could end up being one of the biggest policy challenges in the global economy.

Conclusion

The blame for financial crisis lies with neither governments nor financial markets alone, the caricature extremes visible through the spectacles of the financial gothic. Markets can be inefficient and governments can make mistakes. Generally both happen. The roots of crisis always lie in some mismatch between market forces and government policies, and each episode tends to drive the institutional reforms necessary to restore a rough balance of power. The globalisation of financial markets during the 1980s had run far ahead of both national governments and international bodies. Many national governments had not adjusted to the domestic structural reforms that they would need to withstand financial shocks from the international markets, for example to the minimum international banking standards and principles of accountancy they would have to adopt. It has taken an upheaval on the scale of the events of 1997–8 to make many governments aware of the consequences of engaging with the global financial markets. It also took a crisis to give them enough impetus against domestic opposition to implement policy changes that flew in the face of local traditions or entrenched interests.

Nor were there international policy responses in place in case of a contagious financial crisis. Rapid reactions, decisive politicians in key places, and luck seem to have helped the US Fed and Treasury Department muddle the world through, but the continuing debate about the right 'international financial architecture', discussed in chapter 4, indicates that nobody thinks trial and error will be satisfactory in future. The hunt is on for a structure, and a set of modernised institutions, that suit the conditions of today's global economy as well as the Bretton Woods system fitted in the post-war years. It is pretty clear that globalising international economic institutions is not going to be easy – especially as there is nothing like the institutional vacuum or the sense of urgency that existed in 1945. Unlike the big banks and investment funds, the institutions have to balance explicitly competing sets of national interests. They are inherently political yet can only calibrate national interests by pretending to be nothing more than obedient bureaucracies.

Meanwhile there are vocal demands, not least on the part of the nascent world opposition movement, for tougher restrictions on the financial markets. The next chapter looks at how desirable and how practicable these might be.

2

Myths and Reality in Financial Markets

One academic writing late in 1998 about the financial tempest recalled a speech once given by Woody Allen to a group of graduating students: 'More than any other time in history, mankind faces a crossroads. One path leads to despair and utter hopelessness. The other to total extinction. Let us pray we have the wisdom to choose correctly.'[1]

That just about summed it up for many in the policy community. The menu of options for reform appeared pretty unpalatable. And the more so because the crisis had caught so many of them unawares. The Asian Tigers had been the pre-eminent success story of the international financial markets. The bulk of the huge upturn in private investment in developing countries since the end of the 1980s had been directed towards just a handful, countries like Thailand and Korea prominent amongst them. They had experienced exceptional economic growth and were pursuing essentially stable, orthodox macroeconomic policies. Right up until the time of the Thai devaluation in July 1997, few people had any doubts about the underlying economic success of the affected countries or about the wisdom of investors from capital-rich countries with ageing populations investing in dynamic, young, emerging economies. These structural conditions did not change;

whatever prior structural difficulties existed in the banking system or property market, the source of the upheaval lay in the financial markets.

The conventional economic argument for free international capital markets is based on efficiency and mutual benefit. Investors will be able to seek the highest return (in theory adjusted for risk) on their money, and the highest return will be generated where the potential for growth is greatest. Developing countries will, in turn, gain access to a large pool of funds for investment at a lower cost than if they had to rely on domestic savings alone. Although their paths of development were not as uniform as is often assumed, all of the Asian 'Tiger' populations saved a lot anyway. Still, there is no doubt that their economic growth was speeded and sustained thanks to the free inflow of foreign investment funds. One often-cited study (by Dani Rodrik) found no link between capital liberalisation and the growth rate in developing countries;[2] but others find a positive relationship: in other words, that countries with fewer restrictions on overseas investment did have a higher growth rate. It is hard to believe that the introduction of manufacturing capacity in Asia, for example, by foreign multinationals had no benefits and did nothing to turn the South East Asian economies into 'Tigers', which transformed living standards utterly within a generation.

Most important was direct foreign investment by multinationals, which transferred technology and know-how as well as finance. For one thing, direct investment tends to be longer term; it is a bigger decision to close a factory than to sell some shares. The human results could actually be the same, but it is harder for the distant decision-makers to avoid responsibility for them in the former case. The knowledge characteristics also make direct investment, the building and opening of production plants and offices by overseas corporations, far preferable to the 'hot money' flows of foreign investment in bond and stock-markets, and to overseas bank lending to domestic companies. However, the distinction has until recently been glossed over by advocates of liberalised cross-border investment.

Liberalisation in the international capital markets anyway seemed during the 1980s a natural follow-on from domestic liberalisation and successive rounds of reductions in import tariffs which had enormously boosted world trade to the great benefit of all countries participating in it. Although the tightly regulated post-war economies had experienced what in retrospect turned out to be a golden age of rapid growth, chance and one-off factors also played a big part – a technological catch-up after the war, the baby boom, the role of the US in actively rekindling growth elsewhere, on top of the steady resumption in trade and capital flows after the disruptions of war. Subsequently, planning and direct government interventions proved less and less able to deliver improvements in living standards. On the contrary, the high inflation that ultimately resulted from the macroeconomic policies of the time, the conventional Keynesian consensus, eroded living standards for a majority of citizens. Inflation is a vote-loser, and the stagflation in the 1970s paved the way for the political revolution led by Thatcher and Reagan. Their intellectual legacy has been profoundly important.

The rhetoric and ideology of neo-liberalism remains controversial, to say the least. The election of left-of-centre governments in much of the industrialised world, followed by the global financial crisis, has now sent the high theory of free markets into retreat. But the commitment to market-based economic policies remains, not least because of the convincingly comprehensive collapse of the communist economic system in the watershed year of 1989. As Barry Eichengreen has put it, 'Decades of hard experience have convinced even the graduates of the French Grandes Écoles that markets know better than governments.'[3]

The turning of the intellectual tide in favour of free-market economics starting some twenty years ago was reinforced by the fact that the limits of the process of catching up to the best in US technology had long since been reached. For every other country in the developed world, seeking to adopt the best in US technology and industrial organisation gave plenty of scope for growth in earlier decades. After all, European labour productivity levels were less than half those prevailing in the US in 1945, and Japanese productivity was even lower. Now that a good deal of that catch-up has been accomplished by other developed countries, future growth is a matter of innovation, whether technological or organisational. Governments were bad enough at picking winners; they are truly awful at innovation.

It is a myth that some clever governments got it right: Japan's famous Ministry for Trade and Industry backed all sorts of industrial dodos while ignoring the consumer electronics on which the country's phenomenal post-war growth was built. Sony, for one, was built despite, not thanks to, the MITI. The spirit of entrepreneurship simply does not beat in the bureaucratic breast. More important, governments and their agencies are too distant from the mass of information signalled by market prices and conditions.

Free markets matter more than ever for future growth for a further reason: the nature of the technological changes currently being embodied in all industrialised economies. The new technologies in themselves make it increasingly hard to monitor and control flows of finance and services, and often regulators or even financial institutions themselves can only estimate the amounts of money crossing national boundaries. Computers, the Internet, cheap fixed-line phone calls, mobile phones – these technologies not surprisingly encourage constant communication and the rapid flow of information. It is impossible to see any way of turning the clock back on these developments.

In addition, the further the embodiment of the technology progresses, the more weightless or intangible economic value becomes: material accounts for an ever lower share of the price we pay, and the creative or intellectual content an ever higher one. Financial markets themselves are inherently weightless, their products transferred in huge amounts at little cost and great speed electronically. *Daily* flows in the foreign exchange markets amount to about a tenth of the world's *annual* GDP. The more complex and intangible economic value becomes in the increasingly weightless world, the steadily more impossible it will become to replace or bypass the market mechanism. For nothing transmits information more effectively than the free market. Direct public sector participation in the economy proved problematic even in the relatively simple post-war decades. It has no place in the global transfer of ideas that makes up a growing proportion of modern industry.

One consequence of weightlessness is the often-noted phenomenon of increased trans-national production. Multinationals can more easily shift or subcontract manufacturing to the cheapest developing country location, especially in cases, like Nike shoes, say, or Dell computers, where the profit is all in the brand and the distribution and marketing.

These shifts in production are controversial. Jobs in manufacturing are axed in the home country while the company is suspected of exploitation in the locations to which it has shifted to reduce costs. It is a sort of virtual immigration – the work goes to the source of cheap labour, enabled by information technology and communications, if the cheap labour cannot come to the work, as occurred in the late nineteenth-century version of globalisation. The net effect on overall developed country employment is ambiguous in theory, and many anti-globalists want to believe evidence, like that produced by Adrian Wood (himself a firm critic of protectionism), that it is damaging in practice.[4]

The controversies have perhaps limited the extent to which weighty manufacturing production has moved offshore. In some developed countries, like the US and France, unions are strong enough still to have created effective political obstacles to 'delocalisation'. Yet it could go much further, to the potential gain of both industrialised and industrialising countries. Such shifts in production create the scope for higher-value economic activities in both places. The poorer country certainly gains from the creation of new jobs and the technical and managerial know-how passed on by the investor. The richer country, meanwhile, can gain on average if new jobs replace those exported to the poorer country.

The evidence is that both sets of countries do indeed gain. Wages paid by multinationals and their subcontractors are usually higher than those paid by local employers, and employment in the formal sector tends to rise in the developing countries on the receiving end of the investment. And, certainly, developing countries compete vigorously for these jobs. In the developed countries exporting capital, meanwhile, manufacturing employment contracts; yet the industry remaining at home displays higher levels of labour productivity. Moreover, both the US and UK – with the lowest manufacturing shares in

GDP in the industrial world and big exporters of manufacturing jobs and capital – have low unemployment and
record employment rates. There is therefore little direct
evidence of net job losses due to trade and investment
overseas, although it is certainly true that changing industrial structures in the North due to trade, like the decline
of traditional textiles, have led to massive change in the
type of jobs available. The vast majority of academic
research cannot find any effect that is significant in size.
Less sophisticated objections make the mistake of assum-
ing that there is only a given number of jobs to go around
– the 'lump of labour' fallacy is one of the most frequent
examples where 'common sense' about economics is completely false. It is not true that if a British factory fires 500
workers because it is transplanting a factory to a cheaper
location then there are automatically 500 fewer jobs in the
British economy. For growth, in part boosted by trade, is
what generates new jobs, even if they are in different
industries.

Even so, large-scale industrial restructuring enabled by
technology and by deregulation of markets is bound to be
controversial. Britain has lost entire industries like textiles
to third world producers. The daughter of two textile
workers, I'm nevertheless delighted by the demise of the
industry in the UK. Factory work is boring, noisy, danger-
ous, depressing, thoroughly unpleasant. When the cotton
mills closed between 1978 and the mid-1980s their card-
ing machines, mules and looms went straight into the
textile museums and heritage centres. It is exactly where
they belonged. It is good for us to be able to employ
people outside the mills – working in a call centre would
not suit all of us but it is a much better job than most of
the factory jobs that have been displaced. Commentators
who describe call centres as battery farms or assembly
lines have obviously never been into a real factory. Nor a

call centre. And if poorer countries want their own factories instead, they obviously think it's good for them to industrialise, for the jobs and the export revenues, and all the fruits of development that we have already enjoyed.

This, anyway, is the potential of global free markets, which create winners and losers everywhere but can also produce large net gains. The reality is mixed – but, I argue, less favourable than it could be if opponents of the status quo contested it seriously and pragmatically rather than rejecting out of hand the entire international free-market order.

Global negatives

Markets need good regulation and a robust institutional and legal framework. In addition there are various types of market failure which call for government intervention. This is uncontroversial; debate concerns the details and practicalities. The kind of financial instability inherent in globalised financial markets described in the previous chapter is a problem that existing structures could not tackle well. Those structures clearly need strengthening. In a recent speech Paul Volcker, a former chairman of the US Federal Reserve Board, described it this way: 'Small and open economies are inherently vulnerable to the volatility of global capital markets. The visual image of a vast sea of liquid capital strikes me as apt – the big and inevitable storms through which a great liner like the USS United States of America can safely sail will surely capsize even the sturdiest canoe.'[5] Chapter 4 looks at the detailed reforms and regulatory interventions that are needed.

Global free markets bring other drawbacks along with their benefits, however. Here are some of the other problems – just a few. The powers of those multinational corporations playing international chess with factories and jobs, for one thing. It is perfectly sensible to be all in favour of the reallocation of manufacturing production between developed and developing countries yet concerned about monopoly power and about an imbalance of power between large corporations and national governments. Governments of poor countries that want access to the technology are in a weak bargaining position.

One issue is whether competition for investment is allowing big corporations to play off governments against each other in a successful effort to get their tax bills down. This concerns all governments. Some big multinational corporations operating in the US and UK are well known for their success in limiting their tax bills, entirely legally, through clever internal transactions. Members of the OECD and EU are actively trying to eliminate harmful tax competition between governments. Some conservatives call it harmonisation, and oppose it on the pretext that it is a cover for tax increases; but the aim is nothing more nefarious than preventing corporate citizens from avoiding their fair share of the national tax burden by trading off national jurisdictions against each other. For the alternative to this kind of vigilance is a rising share of the burden falling on labour, relatively immobile compared to capital, with adverse consequences for incomes and job creation.

Other aspects of corporate behaviour cause more concern in developing countries. The question is whether multinationals can get away with applying lower standards of corporate responsibility in poorer countries. Clearly they will pay lower wages in Indonesia than in the US. This is sometimes seen as exploitative in itself, but there is a misunderstanding of basic economics behind the objection to 'offshore' production. The developing country only gets the investment in the first place because wages are lower. Yet the main reason wages are lower is because labour productivity is lower. The people taking the jobs are less skilled and are not exact substitutes for the people who might have worked for that employer in a developed country. They will produce less per hour and of a lower quality.

To the extent that the company is still getting a bargain, paying local employees less than their productivity justifies, it will be joined by competitors who will bid up local wage rates. This is exactly the experience in the South East Asian economies. They became very popular locations as an export base for western companies because of the availability of suitable employees – as well as tax breaks – and so local pay climbed rapidly. It made the multinationals very popular employers. In some countries they offered the one sure route out of grinding rural poverty, and provided women with their best chance of economic independence and the access to better health and even life that come with it. In other countries multinational investors have created for the first time an urban middle class. This is exactly why the Tigers enjoyed such spectacular growth in living standards in the 1980s. This aspect of multinationals' behaviour is economics, not exploitation.

Other labour practices are more problematic, however. Clearly some corporations – or perhaps more often their arm's-length subcontractors – treat employees atrociously. Minimum labour standards have become an important issue, with some campaigners keen to include such requirements in international trade rules. Reasonable people have no trouble agreeing that it is not acceptable for children to work in factories rather than go to school. Big western corporations do not want to hire children anyway – they have their own ethical standards too. But sometimes they use local subcontractors who do employ children because it is cheaper. The question is whether writing a ban on child labour into the international rules would help or harm, or would be more helpful than the genuine vigilance of most big companies against the employment of children anywhere in their chain of supply.

The representatives of developing countries in international organisations are opposed to formal minimum labour standards. One immediate question for them is: what happens to families who get essential cash income from their children's jobs? Ending child labour is part of a broader national development problem requiring a national solution, just as it was a century ago in the developed world. The governments concerned would love incomes to be high enough to eliminate the problem at a stroke, but they have to get to that stage, probably by exporting cheap goods successfully to the rest of the world. Blocking their exports would do little for the children. Other aspects of labour standards, like the use of prison or slave labour, are less problematic.

The thing that makes developing countries really uneasy about the idea of trade rules setting minimum labour standards, though, is that it is the natural protectionists in the North who favour them. It is Northern unions in shrinking industries who most like the idea of penalising countries where children work in factories by restricting imports from them. A coalition of unions with environmental groups destroyed the chance of a new round of trade liberalisation talks this side of the US presidential elections, as the struggling campaign of Vice-President Al Gore needed union money and support. President Clinton torpedoed hopes of an agreement in Seattle by announcing he would like to see trade penalties imposed on the exports of developing nations. Before this concession to union interests, a compromise on taking forward discussions of minimum labour standards had been agreed tentatively between developing and other developed countries.

Child labour and slave labour are flag bearers for other requirements these lobbyists would like to introduce that would make it harder for developing economies to compete for investment. There is simply no convincing evidence that imposing standards of employment more like those prevailing in the rich countries would help the poor countries, although they would almost certainly help defend some kinds of job in the traditional industrial, unionised sectors in the North.

The same is true of environmental standards. Again, nobody in their right minds wants unscrupulous corporations to be able to despoil countries too poor to object to pollution or the exploitation of resources because they so desperately need the jobs. There have been many examples of such a cavalier approach to 'cheap' lives, like the disaster in Union Carbide's plant at Bhopal, and even one is too many. Yet, contrary to received wisdom, multinationals often introduce higher standards of safety and environmental concern than prevail locally, even if just pale imitations of the practices at home. And environmental standards are something that should be set by governments for themselves in negotiation with each other rather than added on to the world's trading rules. Every developing country does now face domestic political pressure to improve environmental standards and has international treaty obligations to do so. As with labour standards, economic growth will be the most effective solution. Concern for the environment amongst citizens is greatest in the richest countries, where people have the fewest worries about the basics like food and shelter. Even within the club of rich countries, those with the wealthiest populations have the strongest and most popular green movements: environmental activism is a luxury good.

This is not to say there is no place for international agreement on the environment. After all, pollution in one part of the planet spills over national borders. Agreements like those limiting emissions will be increasingly important. Environmental issues crop up at the heart of many bitter trade disputes. Take food safety, where trade in British beef can be banned on health grounds according to the rules but trade in US hormone-enhanced beef cannot. Labelling goods by country of origin may be one way out of such inconsistencies, although it puts the burden of complex decision-making on to consumers as well as allowing them a free choice. But labelling, too, is a policy option contested by countries like the US that see it as a trade barrier.

In neither area, environmental or labour standards, is it appropriate to try to impose a specific set of standards on countries when it is not at all obvious how they could achieve them. To argue that the debate concerns setting standards for multinationals rather than standards for other nations is entirely spurious. This is why policy-makers and many intellectuals in developing countries are uneasy about the concerns of campaigners from the rich countries. They see, rightly, a different form of imperialism.

The support for such standards amongst campaigners is actually a political response to the fact that business interests have already successfully imposed similar external rules on developing countries in an abuse of the framework of world trade. Trade-related intellectual property rights (TRIPs) are an obvious and glaring example. The agreement on TRIPs sets minimum standards for the protection of patents, copyrights and trademarks, its aim ostensibly to protect inventors in order to create the conditions for continuing innovation. The rationale for patents and the like, after all, is that without any restrictions on immediate imitation, there would be no incentive for anybody to invent the next big thing. However, the trade agreement on intellectual property essentially gave rich countries some billions of dollars' worth of monopoly profits. For example, it raised the price of pharmaceuticals, typically produced by foreign-owned multinationals, sold in developing countries which had always given drugs weaker patent protection. The incalculable harm done can be summarised by the example of increasing prices for anti-AIDS drugs in Africa. Prices between countries with strong and weak patent protection for pharmaceuticals – Malaysia and India – showed differentials of up to 767 per cent. Likewise, agreement on trade-related investment measures (TRIMs) requires the phasing out of local content requirements, ostensibly on the grounds of levelling the global playing field. Hard to criticise in theory, but harmful in practice to the interests of developing countries.

It would be similarly undesirable for US multinationals to use trade rules to force other countries to accept import of genetically modified foods. National health and cultural concerns make food safety an issue that must be handled delicately in the trade arena. Forced harmonisation in this area would be inappropriate, not at all necessary for the operation of global markets. Allowing detailed labelling of origins, which has so far been seen as a restriction on free trade, may be the right way forward. After going to the brink of a bitter trade row on GM foods and crops on behalf of some of its big businesses, the US has retreated, apparently because it has so little support from other OECD governments.

These examples of the problems arising out of globalisation are not, though, good arguments for introducing a countervailing set of externally imposed rules on the developing world or for trying to roll back free world markets. They are arguments for contesting the shape globalisation takes, which depends on the institutional and regulatory context. I have suggested that some of the developments presented as an inevitable part of global free markets are no such thing, and actually harm poorer countries. Equally, some of the measures proposed on the grounds they will help tame damaging manifestations of market forces could be equally harmful. In both types of case it is not the market process itself that is damaging.

Besides, there is no stuffing the market genie back in the bottle. It is undesirable and impossible. Let's start with the impossibility.

No going back

Quite a lot of modern technological advances are a bit like nuclear power: an incredible force for human good used wisely, potentially catastrophic and impossible to unlearn. At least computers and telecommunications are less literally earth-shattering than either splitting the gene or splitting the atom. On the other hand, they are having quite staggering effects on our economies and societies. They are restructuring industries on a global scale, fuelling the development of new services and products, in a wave of creative destruction. They are changing shopping habits, working time and living patterns. They are even reshaping the urban landscape as new buildings and patterns of urban rise and decline respond over time to these social and economic forces.

There are some ways in which the technologies make it easier for holders of authority to monitor everybody. Closed-circuit television has spread to almost every town centre, and also inside many offices and public buildings. Employers are able to monitor every last keystroke made by employees at their terminals. Companies can collect information about visitors from websites, and computer programs can invisibly mark documents. The gathering of information about individuals on-line by government and private agencies obviously raises concerns about privacy.

Yet the impact of computer technology is in practice exactly the reverse of this nightmare of a virtual panopticon. It is becoming impossible for those in authority to monitor everything. There is too much information; control of everything is out of the question. This applies to financial markets as much as anything. They represent the apogee of computer-aided liberalisation.

Part of the reason is simply the scale of the information that would need to be collected and used. Think about those CCTV cameras. They capture every moment on video but the security guards do not look at every moment, only a random selection of them. If a crime is committed, the tapes can be played through. But they are only kept for a short time before being wiped and reused. To keep the whole of the taped past for a long time into the future would involve record-keeping of Borgesian proportions. Digital technology is making storage, search and retrieval of information vastly easier. But even this technological facility will not create additional incentives to keep track of all the information – why bother?

There is a scale effect in financial markets too. Daily turnover in the currency markets is estimated at $1.3 trillion. These figures are collected through a three-yearly survey of the banks operating in the main financial centres. The banks are required to keep certain records for regulatory purposes, in particular taping conversations between sales staff and customers and making a daily estimate of their 'exposure' in different sorts of currencies and financial assets. They also each day settle their transactions so that the books balance overnight. In other words, there is a lot of detailed information available to senior managers within banks and to national banking supervisors. But national regulators co-operate to an imperfect degree, mainly through international fora such as the Bank for International Settlements and the International Organisation of Securities Commissions.

This does not even take account of the fact that some large players in the financial markets operate from offshore banking centres whose attraction is their secrecy. Hedge funds fall into this category, mostly registered in places like the Caymans or the British Virgin Islands. It is already hard to persuade such centres to hand over enough information to track international crime effectively, so they are unlikely to chase away legitimate investment business by reporting on it too closely. Regulators can only get at the hedge funds at one remove, by their supervision of the banks that do business with them.

More fundamentally, there is no sense in which any single authority can 'know' what is happening in the financial markets because there is too much to know. Even the highest degree of co-operation and a huge effort to collect statistics could only give the big picture without filling in all the detail. There are too many transactions for the authorities sensibly to monitor all of them individually.

Derivatives transactions give the financial markets an additional peculiar freedom from oversight. One characteristic is their complexity; many of the 'over-the-counter' derivatives customised by banks for particular clients are hard to understand. Secondly, derivatives trades are 'off-balance sheet', or, in other words, not recorded in the same way that a straightforward sale or purchase of a financial instrument would be, because the underlying assets from which they are derived are recorded. Accounting for the derivatives too would involve double counting. Thirdly, it is not always clear to anybody what the value of a derivative is anyway. It is not the value of the underlying financial instruments, although related to it. It actually depends on minute-by-minute fluctuations in the financial markets. The banks themselves can only estimate the value, using methods that have become accepted by convention in the financial markets.

Derivatives are simply inherently unmonitorable on any collective scale. But that is almost beside the point compared to the fact that they are also far more useful and therefore more widely used than most people realise. For example, suppose my pension fund manager decides that it would be wise to invest less in US shares, because of the danger of a Wall Street crash, and more in the Japanese stockmarket instead. To sell the US shares and buy the Japanese ones would take time, cost a lot in brokers' commissions, and in the case of a big pension fund might actually move the market prices adversely, dampening the price of the shares being sold simply because of placing its big sell order. It is faster, cheaper and easier to make the switch – or do something that has the same effect – by trading instead in the large and liquid market for index futures, that is, buying and selling units of a share price index at certain dates in the future. Investment managers and corporate treasurers as well as financial traders and speculators rely on the derivatives markets in a daily, bread-and-butter way.

The existence of derivatives means financial market re-regulation would for the most part become unacceptably costly and intrusive. If the authorities decided they would outlaw certain kinds of transaction, they would have to have the creativity to outlaw all the potential derivatives that could mimic those transactions and the powers to demand and process all the information that might be relevant. Take a ban on removing funds out of the country – one type of capital control. Relatively little money leaves in the form of suitcases of cash. (That is hard enough to control, as the case of illegal flows of cash from Italy across the Alps to Swiss banks shows.) The ban amounts to forbidding the sale of domestic currency to buy foreign currency in the main money centres. But it is easy using derivatives to appear to hold domestic currency assets and swap them into another type of asset – if costly because of the need to find a counterparty to the transaction.

During the financial crisis of 1997–8, the Malaysian government imposed restrictions on the flow of capital out of the country. These worked to a fair degree. They could not eliminate capital flight altogether, but many investors did not bother to pull out their funds because the controls were expected to be temporary. However, the restrictions were also very effective at driving away any foreign capital that might otherwise have flowed to the country autonomously.

Other types of controls work rather better. From the early 1990s to September 1998, the Chilean government temporarily required any bank or company investing money in the country to deposit a certain proportion of it with the authorities for a fixed period. It discouraged short-term speculative inflows very successfully for a time without discouraging long-term investment. There were no limits on capital leaving the country. The scheme is seen as a model for emerging economies in the future, as a modest protection against future bouts of financial turbulence. It can keep out the frothiest, most speculative funds. However, the Chilean government suspended the scheme because there was so little appetite for international investment that any marginal discouragement was too much. They wanted the inward investment more than they wanted to retain the control.

Moreover, this kind of holding-period tax on short-term capital flows is something that developed economies do not need because they have a prudently supervised and well-managed domestic financial system, because their banks and financial institutions have pretty good (although obviously not infallible) risk management practices, and because they run macroeconomic and exchange rate policies that do not destabilise the inflows and outflows of capital. This kind of robust and well-regulated financial system should be the ultimate ambition of emerging markets. When they get to that stage, restrictions become superfluous.

The international financial authorities have now accepted, in the wake of the events of 1997 and 1998, that there is a good case for the 'orderly' liberalisation of capital markets, and that Chilean-type controls can be a useful tool. The IMF has tacitly admitted that in the enthusiasm to liberalise investment, it made mistakes, and has pulled back from its earlier gung-ho enthusiasm for rapid liberalisation. It could go further and make it plain, notably to the US authorities, that the purpose of deregulating financial markets in emerging economies is not to create new and profitable business for the American banking industry but rather to improve the efficiency and stability of the financial system.

The recipient governments, under the IMF's eye, made mistakes too. Most emerging markets welcomed the inherently unstable 'portfolio' flows of investment in the stockmarket or short-term bank loans, while restricting or tying up in red tape direct investment by foreign companies. For example, very many still forbid foreign investors to own the majority share of any company, or block takeovers by overseas corporations. But this is good, stable foreign investment that transfers knowledge and opens up export markets. If countries want to liberalise slowly, and

retain some restrictions, it is the more speculative investment and lending these must apply to.

The superiority of direct investment over other forms
can be exaggerated. After all, much of the overseas finance
that built rail and telegraph networks in Latin America,
India and Africa more than a century ago was portfolio
investment in shares. Still, the crises of the 1990s make it
pretty clear that capital liberalisation must be ordered
differently from now on: first direct investment, then
investment in shares and bonds in local companies, and
finally loans by foreign banks. Barry Eichengreen notes:
'This advice would seem obvious but for the large number
of governments that have failed to heed it.' In 1996, just
before the Asian crisis began, an IMF survey found that
144 out of 184 countries placed limits and restrictions of
some sort on foreign direct investment. Eichengreen concludes that these restrictions must be the first to go, before
any further deregulation of the financial markets. 'Several
decades of experience with currency and financial crises
have shown that the best way of learning to swim is not
by jumping in the deep end of the pool.'[6]

The size and fluidity of the financial market undermine
the argument for a tax on speculative capital flows, the so-
called 'Tobin Tax', after Nobel laureate James Tobin,
who argued for a bit of 'grit in the wheels' of the runaway
markets. A low enough and simple enough tax on certain
transactions would not be worth the bother of avoiding.
The biggest banks in the main financial centres are not
law breakers. They would pay up, and it might even
reduce the amount of trading they did. But a low Tobin
tax would not fundamentally alter the balance between
the supposedly good transactions financing trade and
direct investment, which form a very small proportion of
the total, and the supposedly bad short-term investment
and speculation. After all, transaction costs and commis-

sions on investments in emerging markets are high –
higher by many multiples than any proposed tax rate –
and still did not discourage the flow of hot money investment into many countries.

Nobody is in fact seriously proposing a tax high enough
to shut down or shrink the financial markets on such a
large scale. That would be disastrously inefficient and
socially costly, like any tax designed to alter basic patterns
of human behaviour. All taxes shift patterns of behaviour
to an extent but few are designed explicitly as tools of
social engineering. A Tobin tax could be seen as the
financial equivalent of a 'sin tax' like tobacco duty; at the
margin citizens will buy fewer cigarettes, but if it became
too onerous, hardened smokers, including the normally
law-abiding, will get around it, just as too high a tobacco
duty makes cigarette smuggling commonplace.

In addition the practicalities make it a pretty fruitless
exercise – the cost of administration, the international co-
ordination required to share out revenues, and so on.
Taxes are not normally collected internationally, and the
exceptions involve exceptionally coherent groups of
countries like the EU. Think of the amount of controversy
aroused by any European tax proposal, like the suggested
withholding tax, for example, and multiply it up to the
level of the UN. The Tobin tax would just not be worth-
while for a tiny reduction in an extremely large amount of
financial activity. The proposal is unlikely to vanish from
the wish-list of the critics of international free markets,
but no government will waste any political capital at all in
the international arena fighting for it.

The joy of speculation

Turning to the second issue, whether or not a retreat from market forces would be desirable, the idea of capital controls or a Tobin tax presumes that speculation is inherently bad, a source of instability. But no less an authority than Keynes thought it served a valuable economic purpose. In the *Tract on Monetary Reform* he said blaming speculators for volatility was like a witch-doctor blaming illness on the evil eye:

> The successful speculator makes his profit by anticipating, not by modifying, existing economic tendencies. . . . When the type of professional speculation that makes use of the forward market is exceptionally active and united in its opinion, it has proved roughly correct and has, therefore, been a useful factor in moderating the extreme fluctuations which would have otherwise occurred.[7]

After all, futures markets, which trade the most fundamental types of financial derivatives, exist because they could moderate the instability of prices and supplies in food production and basic commodities. The first futures protected farmers from disastrous fluctuations in their incomes and consumers from disruptions in food supply. Without speculators who are willing to take risks, cautious producers would be unable to hedge their own risks.

Keynes went on to criticise foreign exchange restrictions. Too easy to evade and tending to encourage a black market, for one thing. (George Soros agrees, for the same reason.) But more important, they prevent necessary financial market arbitrage, Keynes argued. In other words, he thought speculators lance financial boils. They burst bubbles that need to be burst (although with any bubble there is a puzzle about why they develop and persist in the first place if they are so obviously ripe for bursting). For example, the fact that Soros bet so heavily in the autumn of 1992 that sterling would devalue, costing the UK billions of pounds in the ultimately futile defence of the level of the exchange rate, is something that helped turn him into the symbol *par excellence* of successful and therefore damaging speculation. In popular wisdom, it proved both how good he is and how damaging is his business. However, he was not alone in thinking the pound was overvalued. On the contrary, most of British industry agreed with him. So, at least with hindsight, did the entire political establishment. Most would agree that in the end so-called 'Black Wednesday' did the British economy a great favour. The only lasting damage turned out to be that inflicted on the Conservative Party in its landslide defeat in May 1997.

Even with their attendant instabilities, the growth of global markets is a positive trend. In a recent book, Amartya Sen, the Nobel Prize-winning economist, defends free markets as a device that acts for the interests of the majority against the protected interests of narrow elites. It is an understanding of the benefits of freedom that he traces back to Adam Smith. What's more, the benefits of free markets are diffuse, meaning potential supporters are widely dispersed whereas the benefits of restrictions are often concentrated in an easy-to-mobilise vested interest. Free markets are distinct from other parts of the Thatcherite or Reaganite agenda such as shrinking the role of government in social welfare or education, and Sen is clear that a genuine commitment to markets as a vehicle for economic freedom is a radical position. He concludes that being 'for' or 'against' markets in the abstract is nonsensical; they can have very good results but they can

also be very perverse. 'There is no escape from the necessity for critical scrutiny.'[8]

Long-run growth depends on many factors, some as
fundamental as climate and long-established cultural traditions. Yet although they are not enough by themselves,
international openness and integration into the world
economy have formed the principal path to economic
growth and increased human well-being. At various times
in history and for various countries, an opening up to the
rest of the world has been the catalyst for a burst of
growth, and, conversely, periods of closure have proved
economically damaging. A period of unprecedented globalisation ought to be a time of unprecedented opportunity
and optimism for countries that have not yet benefited
from international economic integration. There is a terrible defeatism in arguments that developing countries
should seek to disengage from the international economic
order, and terrible arrogance also on the part of critics of
capitalism who do not want others to enjoy the same
benefits as consumers that they have experienced
themselves.

Openness is more important than ever because of the
nature of current technological change. It places a high
premium on the free exchange of ideas because ideas form
an increasing part of economic value. In a paper on the
knowledge-based economy, Danny Quah gives the
example of China's turning its back on world trade in the
fifteenth century, fossilising the country's technological
know-how.[9] It was a policy decision possible because the
state had controlled technical progress. There was no
private sector enterprise to fill the gap, and the country's
decline was sealed by the Ming Dynasty (1368–1644),
which for more than a century prohibited overseas trade.[10]
China regressed from being the world's technological and
economic superpower, with a lead of several centuries

over Western Europe in skills such as printing and paper or iron-working, to a backward, mediaeval country. The closure to the outside world not only prevented further advance, it meant that existing achievements fell into disuse. Technical leadership is a process not a state, requiring extreme openness to everything foreign. Open-mindedness, trade, investment and travel are crucial.

It is often argued that globalisation in its modern form is, on the contrary, very undesirable because it threatens to overturn the existing social order, local custom and habit. Many authors have expressed this fear. One of the most-often cited is Karl Polanyi, who wrote in *The Great Transformation*: 'To expect that a community would remain indifferent to the scourge of unemployment, the shifting of industries and occupations and . . . the moral and psychological torture accompanying them, merely because the economic effects in the long run might be beneficial, was to assume an absurdity.'[11] J.K. Galbraith places a similar emphasis on the human need for security and order.[12] More recently John Gray has expressed the same idea.[13] The journal *Marxism Today* complains: 'For a quarter of a century, modernity has been characterised by a profound loss of social control consequent on the free-market regime of globalisation introduced from the late 1970s.'[14]

These critics are wrong. More than that, they are reactionary. I have to confess that I fail to see what is so great about the existing social order that it needs preserving. After all, the opposite of social order is not social disorder, it is a different order. And the opposite of disorder is not necessarily order but control.

The frequent lack of clarity in thinking about these distinctions was neatly demonstrated by two consecutive television programmes I happened to watch one evening while writing this book. The first, presented by a right-wing economist, was about the importance of the nuclear family. It used library footage of ants bustling around a colony carrying leaves as an easy visual shorthand for the complex modern social order, the patterns beneath the apparently random busyness. The following programme was about the instability of the financial markets. It used almost identical pictures of busy ants as a visual symbol of the randomness and chaos in global finance.

Disorder is the exception. It lasts for short periods. Nor is there any sign of widespread and lasting disorder, as opposed to periodic crises, in the operation of free markets. In an interview with the BBC in August 1999, George Soros, reflecting on his part in forcing the British currency out of the European Exchange Rate Mechanism in September 1992, said: 'A single government like the British government has virtually no power.' The wealthy businessman, and politician of sorts, James Goldsmith also turned vigorously against the global financial markets and free trade before his death. My hunch is that rich and powerful men like these do not like the idea of the diffusion of power out of hands that they in turn can influence. Because the beauty of free markets, as well as the problem, is that they can indeed be impervious to control by the privileged few. That nobody is in control opens the window to a more democratic global economy than in the past. Engagement in the global economy can in itself introduce order – some of the most persistent social disorder exists in isolated regimes, pariahs such as Somalia, the Democratic Republic of the Congo or Afghanistan.

What matters in governing the world economy is shaping the right sort of order out of disorder. Globalisation is clearly increasing personal economic and financial risks, and reducing the capacity of existing institutions to protect individuals against risk. This explains its political salience. Still, there is something topsy-turvy about progressive thinkers, in particular, defending an earlier status quo which privileged particular elites, even if one of those elites was the traditional urban, male trade unionist controlling access to specific kinds of jobs.

The fundamental driving force behind globalised markets is not technology, nor a right-wing agenda of deregulation. It is the desire of ordinary people to improve their lot. Free markets are desirable because they are free as well as because they are markets. Knee-jerk political reactions are depressing because they admit no light and shade in their analysis. Markets are not always good and the IMF is not always bad. Too often the policy choices involved in achieving more orderly and less crisis-prone financial markets are presented as stark extremes. Either throw away all restrictions on the international financial markets to avoid permanent relegation to the bottom division of the world economy; or halt the process of market liberalisation before it causes any more damage, and try to roll back some of the deregulation that has already taken place. The better path is what some politicians might characterise as a 'third way' but Eichengreen labels, more appropriately, 'the messy middle'. In a complex and changing world, that is the ground where all the best economic policies are to be found.

3

Division of the Spoils

Episodes plucked from the news during the year after the Asian financial crisis reached its climax.

In August 1999, a few weeks after a well-organised protest in the City of London, French farmers in the Aveyron region vandalised a half-built McDonald's in protest at the US decision to impose prohibitive import tariffs on Roquefort cheese. The tariff was in retaliation for a European Union decision to continue banning imports of US hormone-treated beef on health grounds, even though the World Trade Organisation had ruled the EU's action was illegal. A countryside campaign joined forces with extreme left-wingers to launch what the French newspapers soon named 'l'opération anti-McDo'. One commentator noted that the forthcoming annual meeting of the World Trade Organisation offered the opportunity for the radical left to find a new *raison d'être*. The green/left/farming coalition planned a demonstration in front of the Paris Bourse for the month after the McDonald's protest, just as the J18 movement had done in their 'carnival against capitalism' in the City of London a few weeks earlier. Farmers' leader José Bové became a hero of the global opposition to globalisation.

Back across the Channel the same month, Greenpeace protesters had destroyed a test field of genetically modified oil seed rape in East Anglia that had been planted by a US company, AgrEvo. The company said the local community had accepted the test site, and its destruction had been the work solely of professional campaigners. Greenpeace disputed this, also claiming local support. The British government considered whether future GM crop sites should be kept secret (it decided they should not).

In the US, a successful test case was brought against researchers at the University of Missouri Medical Center who had, in 1995, patented the genetic blueprint for turmeric, for use in the healing of wounds. The spice has long been used on wounds in India, a common folk medicine because of its antiseptic properties. But everyday use had been insufficient protection against the filing of a patent which would have allowed its owners to demand a worldwide royalty. The case was won in the early summer of 1998 on the grounds that ancient Sanskrit documents provided satisfactory evidence that turmeric had previously been used for the same purpose. Patents cannot be applied to old discoveries provided there is adequate documentary evidence of past use.

This could not be dismissed as an isolated case. In November 1999 a Japanese company sought a patent for curry. These examples highlight the absurdity of applying one set of legal norms to another culture in this globalised world.

And, of course, at the start of December 1999 there was the riot outside the gathering of the World Trade Organisation in Seattle. Protesters trashed not only the classic symbol of global/US economic imperialism, McDonald's, but also a Gap store and a Starbucks coffee shop. All, needless to say, represent aspects of America that consumers elsewhere in the world are eager to buy as soon as they can afford to.

★

There are countless other examples that could make the same point. The resolution of the global financial crisis was not the end of the story, but rather its beginning. The crisis focused public attention on the process of globalisation. International trade and investment have become a political war-zone.

In the golden decades of growth after the Second World War, the progressive dismantling of trade barriers and exchange controls, stimulating rapid growth in exports and overseas investment, was widely seen as an indisputable good. This is not to say that countries shed all their traditional mercantilist tendencies. All tried to develop national champions, boost competitiveness and corner markets in the traditional way. Still, successive rounds of discussions in the General Agreement on Tariffs and Trade from 1948 culminated in the creation in 1994 of the World Trade Organisation. It had been intended to create this as a key part of the management of the international economy fifty years earlier, alongside the World Bank and International Monetary Fund, but trade had proved too sensitive a subject immediately after the war. Instead the semi-formal GATT rounds stood in for a formal institution. Now that the WTO exists at last, trade has once again become one of the most contentious areas of global economic governance.

The fledgeling institution already stands at a decisive juncture, having failed to launch a Millennium Round of talks to liberalise trade in increasingly sensitive areas such as agriculture, services and also foreign direct investment at the December 1999 annual meeting in Seattle. The real failure in Seattle occurred inside the conference hall, not in the streets. It was caused by a US attempt to shape the trade agenda in its domestic interests, as it always has, ignoring the interests of developing countries. These, empowered for the first time in trade negotiations by the uniquely democratic structure of the WTO, refused to play along.

Nevertheless, the rioters outside grabbed the headlines, and the WTO has become a focus for the backlash against globalisation. And, oddly, the backlash is fiercer in the developed countries, where campaigners accuse their own governments of rigging the world trading and investment system to the advantage of the rich and disadvantage of the poor, than in the developing world. While there are indeed strong grassroots campaigns against the forces of globalisation in some developing countries, they have neither mass nor elite sympathy. Even in South East Asia, rocked by financial crisis, there is no serious questioning of the trading and investment regime. On the contrary, there is more support for the principles of free trade in emerging economies because this free-market rhetoric is exactly what has been opening the rich OECD markets to developing countries over the decades. Countries like the Asian Tigers have experienced massive boosts to living standards, achieved thanks to a policy of exporting their way to prosperity. As Fred Bergsten, the Washington-based trade economist puts it, 'The developing countries have a very strong interest in the outcome of these global economic debates. "Outward orientation" has become a central tenet of virtually every successful development strategy.'[1]

At the inter-governmental level, too, the most serious tensions arise amongst the members of the 'Quad Group' – the EU, US, Japan and Canada – the informal group which directs trade policy. It is not that tensions between developing and developed country governments do not exist. That they do was amply demonstrated by the six-month deadlock over naming the new director general of the WTO, mentioned at the start of this book. Unable to resolve the impasse over whether New Zealander Mike

Moore should succeed to the job, or Thai Supachai Panitchpakdi, the organisation's members eventually decided each should get half a term. However, the most serious disputes to be taken so far to the WTO for resolution have involved the US against the EU or the US versus Japan.

The shape of both the outright backlash against and the disputes within the trading system suggest that something more complex is taking place than a cartoon struggle between oppressive rich and exploited poor. Certainly, there are important battles to be fought to determine the division of power and wealth between multinational companies and indigenous peoples, say, or the corporations and their low-paid workforces in developing countries. Yet at the same time the global system of trade and investment has become the arena for domestic political struggles within the developed world. The controversies have arisen after a period of rising income inequality, stagnant incomes for many at the bottom of the distribution, and apparently unbudgeable unemployment in Continental Europe alongside unprecedented increases in joblessness in Japan. In an increasingly 'winner takes all' economy, there is a growing contrast between winners and the swollen ranks of losers.

It scarcely matters for this kind of distributive tension that there is almost no evidence that the growth in international trade and investment has affected either incomes or employment levels in the OECD countries. In theory, either could increase inequalities between those working in industries exposed to international competition and those working in sheltered industries. And they could reduce employment in the exposed sectors. Whether they do or not is an empirical matter. And a great many studies have found that they have not. Even in the most open economies trade is not big enough to explain more than a

small part of the job losses widespread throughout manufacturing industry. For throughout the developed world
manufacturing output and employment, as shares of the
economy-wide totals, have been in decline since the mid-
to late 1960s. That is long before the earliest beginnings
of the recent accelerated process of globalisation.

One thorough and important work found the other way,
but its author, Adrian Wood, stands pretty much alone in
finding trade a plausible culprit.[2] Essentially, his method
makes the assumption that all of the change in industrial
structure in the OECD over three decades is due to
globalisation. Trade leads to specialisation in higher-
skilled work in the industrialised economies, at the
expense of low-skilled labour. There is obviously some
truth in this, but other factors — mainly technology and
changing patterns of consumer demand as average
incomes have climbed – are bound to have played a big
role too. As Paul Krugman has pointed out repeatedly,
the scale of trade with low-wage countries has never yet
been great enough to account for more than a tiny share
of the decline in manufacturing as a share of the developed
economies. He notes (writing about the US): 'Imports
from low wage countries were almost as large in 1960 as
in 1990 – 2.2 per cent of GDP – because three decades
ago Japan and most of Europe fell into that category. In
1960 imports from Japan exerted competitive pressure on
labor-intensive industries such as textiles.'[3] There are two
far more plausible culprits for this declining share of
manufacturing in output and jobs: increased automation
in industry, and consumer demand shifting towards services. And, of course, US unemployment is once again at
its lowest since the 1960s while in the UK joblessness has
fallen rapidly despite the continuing decline of the manufacturing share in the economy.

However, the aridity of econometric studies makes little

headway against what is popularly believed to be true. Certain politicians have played to the popular, 'common-sense' fears. There have been the classic populists of the right, like James Goldsmith and Pat Buchanan, and left, like Richard Gephardt. More extreme are, on the one hand, the environmentalists and aid campaigners and, on the other, the US radical right, with its paranoid militias seeing everywhere signs of a conspiratorial world government.

The MAI – a dry run

A preliminary skirmish for the great war over the World Trade Organisation was the clash between the OECD and radical campaigners over the Multilateral Agreement on Investment. The MAI was a draft treaty on international investment drawn up for member governments of the OECD – that is, the club of the world's richest twenty-nine countries – to sign. Its aim was to create a level playing field in investment rules within the OECD for national and foreign companies. For example, the OECD governments would not be able to subject foreign companies to local content rules, demanding investors buy a certain proportion of the supplies they needed from within the country, if national companies did not have to abide by the same minimum. So focused were the officials drafting the treaty on the fact that it was intended only for its own members that they paid no attention to the effect it might have on other countries. Protesters were to claim there would be moral pressure on emerging economies to abide by the same rules, which would open them to unfair competition from multinationals, so much tougher and more efficient than local companies. Nor did officials and diplomats consider the possibility that the MAI could be portrayed as a charter for multinationals to exploit the powerless – not realising there would be a propaganda war, the OECD had not bothered with the most elementary defences.

It did not take long, however, for trade union negotiators and environmental campaigners to attack the shape the draft treaty had taken. Ironically, they were ultimately successful in adding to it – before consigning it to the diplomatic pending tray – new clauses concerning minimum environmental and labour standards in international investment. Although not onerous on multinational companies, these would have made the MAI the first international treaty to contain such clauses, setting a potentially valuable precedent. Previously the G7 powers had always insisted that labour standards were a matter for the International Labour Organisation (a branch of the UN) and environmental standards for separate international negotiation. The redrafted MAI would have breached this ring-fencing of trade and investment as pure economic issues to be kept separate from social matters.

How is international investment ever to be regulated if not with a set of legally binding international rules embodied in a treaty? The growing flows of international capital can only be governed if the necessary mechanisms are created and international organisations empowered to apply and monitor them. There will have to be an international investment treaty, which would best be applied through the World Trade Organisation. Unfortunately, it is hard to see how it will be possible to introduce any framework governing cross-border investment if campaigners insist on painting any attempt as son-of-MAI.

Few protesters had bothered to follow the details of the negotiations, which had been obscure to start with and were never reported closely even by specialist journalists. Most continue to refuse to believe that any good at all could have come from the MAI, that somehow as a concept an international investment treaty necessarily involves formalising the powers of multinationals rather than formalising the international powers of governments over multinationals. It is a sure thing that when discussion of international investment arises again in the WTO negotiations, the same coalition will rush to paint it as the MAI by the backdoor, with the Pavlovian reaction that implies. But in this case it is hard to see how there can ever be any rules that will protect emerging economies from the potential free-for-all of global monopoly capitalism. It is a classic Pyrrhic victory of idealism over dirty realism.

The MAI was not to be, however. At the April 1998 ministerial meeting of the OECD, at its headquarters at the Chateau de la Muette in central Paris, a raggle-taggle of protesters gathered in the public gardens on the other side of the wall. A few stalls sold food, a juggler performed, somebody played his tin flute and a handful of protesters stood with placards, idly watched by bored policemen. It was a sad spectacle by comparison with some anti-globalisation protests. However, inside the negotiating chamber, the campaign had achieved a great victory. With the French and American governments getting cold feet about the treaty thanks to domestic lobbying (including lobbying by US corporations), it was kicked into touch by diplomats, never to be revived. 'It's a pity. It wasn't a bad treaty in the end,' one union negotiator said to me as the news emerged. Ironically, unions and campaigners welcomed the agreement, at the OECD's 2000 ministerial meeting, to implement a set of non-binding guidelines for multinational investment. These included core labour and environmental standards. But the WTO remains the only body able to impose binding rules. It is emerging as the new forum for conflict on all the most difficult issues in governing the world economy.

World Trade Organisation on the front line

Most people have never heard of the World Trade Organisation. Most of those who have heard of it hate it. The capers on the streets of Seattle, as protesters tried to disrupt the organisation's annual ministerial meeting in December 1999, brought it wider name-recognition, but a good reputation is going to be an uphill struggle.

The WTO has taken over from the International Monetary Fund as the institution good people love to hate. The Great Satan of globalisation. But it will be a desperate tragedy for the vast number of people living in poverty in this world if the new trade round fails. The campaigners and demonstrators with – mostly – the best of intentions will have done terrible harm to those they claim to help if they establish the idea that trade is bad. Trade is not just the best way, but the only path out of poverty for a developing country. More trade liberalisation is essential.

It is easy to see how the 'trade is bad' notion got off the ground. Start with the WTO's name. 'World' is a lot more arrogant than 'International', and 'Organisation' is a definite no-no across a key swathe of the political spectrum. 'Trade' isn't great either – it conjures up beef and bananas, and is all to do with the numbers always stacking up in favour of the Americans.

However, the WTO has a lot more wrong with it than could be remedied by rebranding. To begin with, it is terribly secretive and bureaucratic, it's overrun by lawyers, and is based in insular Geneva, one of the wealthiest cities in the world. The rich countries call the shots as they have all the lawyers, although that is changing slowly. Moreover, the WTO operates by consensus, which means that all 134 members must agree on everything. For half of 1999 they could not even agree who should run it.

The WTO was also launched into a world that is rapidly growing more complicated. However ill equipped, it has turned out to be the natural forum for some of these modern complexities to come to a head. Can a biotech company be allowed to patent a natural remedy? Is hormone-treated beef safe to sell to consumers? Why should a third world government protect a foreign company from pirate copies of its products? Virtually any conflict across international borders will probably end up as a trade dispute.

Thank heavens for such a forum, then. The WTO is a bit like a sheriff in the Wild West, whose silver star meant authority only if the really tough guys agreed. But at least having a sheriff is an admission of the rule of law. The WTO has replaced the *ad hoc* negotiations that used to take place, where the interests of the least powerful scarcely had any consideration.

We all know that rules tend to favour the powerful, but the fact that in principle they apply to everybody does offer the powerless some protection. An organisation that enforces trade rules is not to be sniffed at when it replaces the earlier international cowboy capitalism of deals between power blocs. The WTO has several times ruled against the two biggest hoodlums, the US and the EU, and not always when they were slugging it out against each other. The Seattle meeting was a landmark event not because of the mayhem in the streets and coffee bars, but because it was the first time that a group of developing countries came to the trade negotiating chamber with a co-ordinated and agreed agenda. Negotiators from the developed countries describe it as a key event in global politics. If it works at the WTO, it will work in the IMF and United Nations in future. Ironically, for the first time the US and the EU were not to be able to get their own way, at the exact moment that a large group of campaigners in the rich countries started to accuse their own governments of an abuse of power.

Confusingly, one of the things that the developing countries are most bitterly opposed to is the US-led plan to impose trade sanctions on countries whose exporters do not meet certain minimum labour standards, including a ban on the use of child labour. Nobody, but nobody, believes that children ought to be at work instead of at school. The labour standards link to trade is, however, inspired by profoundly protectionist US unions.

Those high-profile American campaigns to make consumers feel warm and cosy by boycotting cheap trainers from abroad because of the atrocious conditions of the workers are a sham. Boycotts, like the new proposal to tax certain imports if third world factories cannot meet American standards, punish people for their poverty. The developing countries know that the labour standards issue is all about protecting union jobs in developed markets, and they will not fall for it.

What the poor countries do need is more access to the rich markets and rapid growth in world trade. They need to sell more cheap clothes and food and electronic goods into the protected markets of America and Europe. They need the great powers to live up to the rules laid down when they founded the WTO in 1994.

There are many well-meaning people who challenge the suggestion that international trade is the source of economic growth. They have convinced themselves of something that is wholly wrong. Poor countries become less poor – rich, even – by exporting. Some have, in this way, transformed the living standards of their people within a generation. Study after study has shown that the developing nations as a group have not just benefited from trade, but have done so disproportionately in the sense that they have enjoyed bigger percentage increases in their GDP than have the rich countries.

Ignore, though, the doubling in world GDP per head in the past half century. Suppose it is true that the result of fifty-plus post-Second World War years of trade liberalisation has been unfair. All the more reason to hope that a successful round of trade liberalisation can be salvaged from the débâcle in Seattle. Nothing will change if it is not.

The early signs, in the midst of a US presidential campaign, were that progress would be at best extremely slow, even though a new round of talks on free trade could make a fundamental difference to the livelihood of the poorest people on this one planet of ours. There is a serious danger that we are about to lose an unrepeatable opportunity to afford the developing world an era of growth that will raise hundreds of millions, even billions, of people out of desperate poverty. There is nothing more urgent than the need for the World Trade Organisation to launch a successful new round of trade liberalisation. The attack on poverty is threatened by the coalition of activists who increasingly see any acceptance of globalisation as a victory for US multinationals. Relatively little of their anger applies to French or Swedish or Japanese multinationals – it is rare to see placards against Asea Brown Boveri or Elf. For what they oppose in economic dimensions is the same faultline that splits the globe in other areas: American hegemony, or Barber's Jihad versus McWorld.[4]

This understandable tension casts a cloud of obscurity over trade issues, which are complicated and dull at the best of times. There is no doubt that the US government puts its weight behind the interests of its national companies, which include some of the biggest multinationals.

All countries do this. It is also plain that some strong lobby groups in the US sometimes persuade the administration to take a protectionist stance. Thus the steel industry gets strong backing from official negotiators in discussions with Japan, which is accused of dumping steel at below cost prices in the US market. Again, any government would do this for a forceful, organised lobby. At the same time, the US has in the past, although less so recently, been the single most consistent and rigorous defender of free trade in the world. What's more, it has restricted its own powers in trade policy by signing up to the rules of the WTO, which it did so much to bring into being.

The banana row offers a good example of the facile demonination of the US. In June 1999 the WTO found in favour of the US and against the European Union in a dispute over how many bananas from Latin America could be imported into Europe. The company involved, Chiquita, is a US corporation which has made political donations to both Republicans and Democrats. The EU had restricted Chiquita's imports of Central American bananas in favour of bananas from small producers in African and West Indian countries which were former French and British colonies. It was easy to paint this dispute, therefore, as a big, bad American multinational calling in political favours against heroic smallholders with whom Europe had ties of history and obligation.

However, this was a distortion. The EU had failed to meet an earlier trade agreement to phase out over ten years its preferential treatment of former colonial trading partners. This lengthy protection had removed any incentive for those producers to improve efficiency in order to compete on the open world market, and, with its lifting, West Indian growers now face a painful financial shock. In any calculus of need, both Central American and West

African farmers alike would come out pretty badly – both earn pretty low incomes from banana exports. And Chiquita, while a donor to both political parties in the US, is not a major contributor to either. There would be no point. Bananas just do not carry the same political clout as steel, cars or Midwestern farmers.

There will be more and more disputes of this sort unless the leading governments resolve to rise above them and set in train further global liberalisation in increasingly difficult areas – agriculture, services, and also investment. The momentum is crucial. The history of post-war trade negotiations demonstrates convincingly that standing still is an unstable situation in trade relations. The world has always moved towards either greater freedoms or greater protectionism. Trade experts call this the 'bicycle theory'. Protectionism gained ground after two previous rounds of liberalisation – the Kennedy Round in the late 1960s and the Tokyo Round in the early 1980s. The biggest wave of protectionism, of course, came in the 1930s, cementing or perhaps even causing the Great Depression. A reversal of free trade now would pose a far greater threat to the developed and developing economies alike than the crisis of 1997–8. More important, it would throw away a rare opportunity to tackle poverty in the developing countries. The trend towards increasing global inequality came to a halt in the 1980s as India and China started to liberalise and open up to trade. This demonstrates the potential for increasing the prosperity of the very poor – and the scale of the opportunity that could be wasted.

Unfortunately, there is no great wave of liberalisation on the horizon, no obvious constituency for it, and no political leadership on the subject either. The US has a big trade deficit and the 2000 election campaign cast its shadow over free traders. Japan has turned inward as its economy remains moribund in the long aftermath of the late 1980s boom. In the EU only the UK has reasonably strong free-trade instincts, with the other big member nations far more inclined towards creating Fortress Europe. Crucially, consumer groups rarely make the case for free trade, even though consumers benefit greatly through lower prices and wider choice.

There were two sorts of voices joining in the loud protests in Seattle against global trade, two meanings in the chorus: 'Hey, hey, ho, ho, WTO has got to go!' On the one hand, the well-intentioned campaigners, children of the '68 generation, who think trade rules work against the interests of poor people in developing countries. On the other, the US unions, who want to use labour standards in the developing world as a pretext to protect their own members' interests. Disaffected young dropouts claiming that 'Capitalism Kills' might have been the focus for all the lenses, yet all but 5,000 of the 30,000 or so demonstrators outside the December 1999 meetings were estimated to have been American union members. President Clinton was bowing to the needs of electoral politics when he said the WTO should look at the possibility of trade sanctions against countries which do not meet certain minimum labour standards, including a ban on the use of child labour. Al Gore, his vice-president, needed money and support from the unions in his presidential bid.

In doing so he destroyed the chance of a favourable outcome from the meeting as developing countries, rightly, and angrily, saw through the veil of concern to the cynical protectionist politics. With luck, and away from the TV cameras, there can still be a sensible compromise to create a working group involving the WTO and the International Labour Organisation to look at this vexed question of labour standards. Child labour is abhorrent, there is no doubt about it. But to restrict exports from certain countries because of it would achieve nothing more than punishing them for their poverty, and punishing their poorest people the most heavily.

Lessons of Seattle

The entanglement of the WTO in the labour standards question raises several important points, however. One is just the alarming degree of economic illiteracy in public debate. Politicians are amongst the biggest culprits. Few of them have bothered to insist while the Seattle talks were in progress that the freedom to exchange goods makes for efficient economies, and trade is good for growth. That growth is good for the environment because countries need to put poverty behind them to care. Or that globalisation, by integrating developing countries into the world economy, can be the strongest force for democracy and labour rights.

To the charge that institutions like the WTO and other pantomime villains such as the International Monetary Fund are not representing the interests of developing countries, the correct response would be a reassessment of how the system of international economic governance is working. Which organisations are insufficiently transparent, badly managed or ineffective? The forward march of globalisation is certainly putting demands on the international bureaucracies that they find hard to meet. Their task is made all the harder by the fact that politicians have simply not thought very much about how to represent and balance national interests in a multilateral world. In the case of free trade, national interests need not actually conflict, although sectional ones might do so. Freer access to US markets for third world textiles producers would damage the interests of US unions but consumers everywhere would benefit.

The fact that trade is today's issue is beside the point for the Generation X protesters, though. One year's campaign was the IMF and third world debt, the next's is the WTO and labour standards, and there will be something new the year after that. Like the earlier protest movements, they don't agree about what they are for but they definitely know what they are against. Trade is the easiest focal point of globalisation.

The US trade expert Fred Bergsten wrote in a recent paper: 'Paradoxically, the strongest pressures to reverse the liberal course can be founded in the countries that created, nurtured and championed the postwar order: the United States and the European Union.'⁵ The reason, he argues, along with the far greater openness of the US to trade, is the stagnation of low incomes in the US. Protectionism in both regions is coming in from the cold, with politicians not at either extreme arguing that regional free trade – within the EU or the North American Free Trade Association – makes up for closure to the outside.

To make matters worse, it is getting harder to liberalise because the forms of protection are becoming subtler. For instance, direct investment is now a crucial aspect of trading relations. There will have to be some form of multilateral agreement between developing and developed nations. It will no doubt prove controversial again. Yet new research suggests that rules that appear to protect the poor recipient of direct investment from exploitation – for example, local content rules or formal requirements for the transfer of technology – are counter-productive. They end up discouraging the multinational investor from fully integrating the local subsidiary into its global network.

Other areas will prove equally contentious. Dismal labour standards can be used as a form of unfair competition – 'social dumping' – so will need to be discussed in the context of trade. At the same time, cheap labour is the chief competitive advantage of emerging economies, so labour standards certainly could be a backdoor trade barrier.

New controversies

Environmental standards, biotechnology and health concerns such as GM foods look likely to be yet more controversial than social questions like labour standards. The latter can be used by rich countries to create trade barriers and prevent competitors gaining fair market access. Yet it would be wrong to brush aside genuine concerns about environmental or social issues. Nowhere is the removal of boundaries by globalisation more immediate than in the case of environmental and health spillovers. As the scale and extent of interconnection increases, so does its reach, with fewer barriers against pollution or disease brought from elsewhere.

The potential impact of new technological developments, for good or bad, in healthcare or agriculture accounts for a lot of the emotive power of such issues. Nothing matters more than our health or the food we eat. But it is also the apparent power the technologies place in the hands of specific multinationals, mainly American, that makes them so controversial. Biotechnology and genetic manipulation offer enormous promise – cures for terrible diseases or more productive crops free of herbicides and pesticides. Yet steadily fewer of these advances are the result of scientific research in the public domain, and more and more are patented by private companies. For example, most US seed research in the early 1980s was government-funded and patents were rarely sought. But as universities sought research funding from the private sector, the research output became increasingly patented. By 1990 the proportion of public sector patents in biotechnology sold under exclusive licence to a private sector manufacturer had reached 40 per cent.

The private sector must have a role in the commercial development of biotech and genetically modified products. Apart from the importance of market signals in determining which products will be viable because there is a demand for them, without the potential for profit, far less applied research would be carried out. However, it is the concentration of the industry that gives real grounds for concern. The ten biggest corporations have market shares of around a third in seed and pharmaceuticals, 70 per cent in computers, and more than 80 per cent in pesticides and telecommunications. Economies of scale in such research-intensive industries account in part for their growing concentration. Even so, the monopoly power justifiable explains a good deal of the public unease. Public concern (in the developed markets) has turned out to be a powerful weapon in itself. Monsanto, the biggest, baddest producer of genetically modified seed as far as the general public was concerned, has divested itself of its most controversial businesses. Controversy turned out to be too bad for business in this case.

The consumer backlash has been more or less confined to developed markets. But they at least have competition authorities and public health bodies that put real limits on the powers of even the biggest corporation. A more serious matter is the imbalance of knowledge and power between developing country consumers and multinational corporations. The previous chapter noted the unfairness of the WTO agreement on trade-related aspects of intellectual property rights. The number of international patent applications under the multilateral regime soared from less than 3,000 in 1979 to the equivalent of nearly 3.5 million in 1997. Of these patents, 97 per cent are held by the rich countries, and more than half of global licensing fees were paid to the US. What's more, over four-fifths of the patents granted in developing countries belong to residents of the developed countries. According to the United Nations Development Programme, the idea of intellectual property rights is a novelty in developing countries. It argues, in the 1999 *Human Development Report*, that the TRIPs regime will prevent the kind of technological and industrial catch-up that East Asian countries were able to exploit in the 1960s. And not only does it exclude newcomers from the technological frontier, it also fails to recognise traditional knowledge. Thus, in the pharmaceuticals industry, more than half the most-frequently prescribed drugs are derived from plants or synthetic copies of plant material. Yet developing countries, home to the great majority of the world's biological riches thanks to their biodiversity, are unable to harvest the wealth that will flow from this patrimony. Not surprisingly, sixty developing countries had failed to implement the TRIPs accord by the 1 January 2000 deadline, after a five-year phasing-in period. Pakistan had started a bid to renegotiate the agreement. According to the UNDP, there is no difference between a multinational patenting a plant gene and industrial espionage. The report calls it 'theft of both the genetic materials and the long-acquired knowledge of using them to develop medicines.'[6] It says even a low 2 per cent royalty on the use of genetic resources would amount to a transfer of more than $5bn from the profits of the multinationals to developing countries, and suggests 10 per cent would be fairer.

In both its aspects, the imbalance between rich and poor countries, and between producers and consumers in the developed markets, the globalisation of biotechnology puts distributional questions in the spotlight. If it is the case that technical advance benefits consumers, boosts

Division of the Spoils

living standards and makes the world a better place, then this is exactly the arena where the favourable evidence should emerge. Ultimately, globalisation cannot and will not benefit the shareholders in the top fifty high-tech corporations. It is precisely in agreements like the WTO and its TRIPs accord that the distribution of gains will be determined.

Immigration

Its executives might beg to disagree, but the WTO is not the forum for all the contentious issues in economic globalisation. One of the most difficult is immigration, legal and illegal. The scale of migration is one of the big differences between globalisation now and a hundred years ago. Compared to the tides of people who left the Old World for the New (North America, Latin America, Australia and New Zealand) in the late nineteenth and early twentieth centuries, today's flows scarcely register. Immigration into the US amounted to 30 million between 1880 and 1920 and reached about 1.6 million people a year at the pre-First World War high point. Legal inflows to the US climbed back to around 1–1.5 million a year during the 1990s, a high rate but a far smaller proportion of the existing population. Only three countries, the US, Canada and Germany, have seen inflows of immigrants as high as 4–5 per cent of their population in recent times.

The reasons for immigrations have not changed over the intervening century, however. War and famine will always put populations on the move. But it is the chronic desperation of poverty that drives people to abandon their homes, families and friends in the hope of a better life. Or, in dry jargon, economic migration outweighs the flows of political refugees and asylum seekers. In contrast to the decade or two after the end of the Second World War, when labour shortages made many OECD countries accept or even seek large numbers of economic immigrants, the rich countries have now put up uniformly high barriers to legal immigration and redoubled their efforts to police and discourage illegal immigration. This is despite an emerging labour shortage. Not only is there a severe shortage of specific skills, such as computer programming ability, but almost all the rich countries face a looming decline in the ratio of working age to retired population. This poses the threat of a severe problem in financing pension schemes, whose solutions could include higher retirement ages and higher taxes. However, higher immigration would be an alternative.

Yet the political opposition to increased immigration is so high, even in countries where there is very little to start with, that an active policy of drawing in overseas workers is a non-starter. Nevertheless, it is increasingly hard to maintain the fiction that everything can and will be free to flit around the globe except the world's citizens. If free trade and free capital are good things, it is hard to think of plausible reasons why free movement of labour is not.

There are many bogus rationales. Anti-immigrant arguments include myths about the drain immigrants place on welfare and health systems, and about the jobs they 'steal' from residents. On the contrary, first-generation immigrants have been found to make a net contribution to the state, paying more in tax than they claim in benefits and health care. Immigration does lower the average wage in certain areas, but mainly through the net creation of low-wage jobs that would not exist otherwise, because the native-born will not do bad jobs for low pay. A more sensible rationale for at least controlling the inflow of migrants from poor to rich countries is the social one, the need to maintain as far as possible harmonious race relations. There are many practical, transitional difficulties posed by mass immigration too, like the need for housing and additional infrastructure, or language support in schools in specific areas.

Good sense is absent from the immigration debate, unfortunately. There is a political conspiracy of silence about it. Governments in the developing countries never want to admit that things are so bad that large numbers of their people want to give up on their home country and emigrate. Those in the developed countries do not want a hugely controversial subject to appear on the public political agenda, and prefer to continue with a closed-frontier policy, piling on additional police and immigration resources if needed.

But even with heads buried in the sand on a global basis, the 'problem' of immigration will remain and grow. The numbers of people on the move across national boundaries are huge and rising even in the face of high barriers. It is straightforward economics. The flows of people are a function of the growing inequality of incomes. Unless the international community acts fast and effectively to tackle poverty – and the signs are not hopeful, with more than 1.3 billion people living on less than $1 a day – migration pressures will continue to build all around the boundaries of the rich countries. The forces of globalisation do not respect the niceties of wealth and status.

Conclusions

It is the divergence between the promise held out by globalisation, by its official rhetoric of freedom and prosperity, and the benefits being delivered that accounts for the political backlash. The economic gains have so far been unfairly distributed, as reflected in either growing inequality within the rich countries or growing inequality between rich and poor countries. In the public mind there is a suspicion that the process is set up to enrich the already wealthy, whether individuals or multinational corporations.

The balance will have to shift – indeed, the backlash is part of the democratic process that will achieve this. However, it is essential that domestic political conflict in the rich nations is not acted out on the rest of the world. Protesters against the MAI and WTO, in linking their cause to the interests of specific unions, have done exactly this. Their preferred outcome would reinforce the existing chasm between rich core and poor periphery. This focus has diverted effort from aspects of the current trade regime that are obviously against the interests of the developing countries, notably the intellectual property rights regime and its implications for access to both the rewards of traditional knowledge and the promise of new technology.

Other aspects of the opposition to globalisation have been more constructive in terms of seeking a rebalancing of the gains. The successful campaign for improved debt relief, led by Jubilee 2000 (see chapter 4), is one example. (It also, incidentally, demonstrates how hard it has been to achieve even a small shift towards developing countries, having been a long, hard haul with many setbacks.) In the case of debt relief it was also pretty easy to see what was needed and form a coalition around a simple demand, whereas the evidence is more muddled, the analysis much more complicated, and therefore more fiercely contested, in the case of trade.

Yet despite the complexities, the balance of gains from globalisation will have to shift towards today's losers. The world economy cannot be milked for the benefit of a tiny minority for long without generating unsustainable crisis and conflict. The pressure points today will prove an important test of the rhetoric of free markets and global-isation, for they concern issues that will demonstrate in whose interests the global economy is being run. Free trade must be free for everybody, and if trade and capital are free, then people will have to be freer to move as well. The next chapter looks specifically at the institutions of global economic governance, and proposals for their reform, before returning to the broader theme of the contestability of the process of globalisation.

4

A New International Architecture

The institutions governing the world economy were shaped by two forces: the overwhelming political events of the mid-twentieth century, and the vivid memories of the Great Depression. The combination of economic and political cataclysm gave the experts and diplomats meeting in Bretton Woods, New Hampshire, in 1944 an unusually clean sheet of paper on which to sketch out their design. The Cold War froze international political relations for the following forty-five years, giving those Bretton Woods institutions an exceptionally stable framework. The politics of managing the world economy have become far more sensitive and complex since 1990, however. On the other hand, there has been no economic upheaval big enough to generate a consensus for change in what has become known as the international financial architecture, never mind a consensus about what the changes ought to be.

Out of the post-Asian crisis market turmoil have come a series of contradictory, mutually inconsistent analyses and proposals for reform. And the leading economic powers along with the IMF are in no position simply to pick one set of reforms, because decisions must be negotiated in a way that would not have been necessary ten or twenty years ago. So, paradoxically, at the same time that

Washington is more than ever the hegemonic economic power, it is in a weaker position to dictate the institutions governing the world economy. This is reflected in the increasing unwillingness on the part of the US Congress to pay its share in the budgets of these organisations – a gut political reaction that if they can't call the tune, why pay the pipers?

The array of institutions is bewildering to anybody who is not an avid reader of the financial press. There is an alphabet soup of organisations, and they are multiplying. It is worth giving a brief outline of the most important.

Key decisions are taken by the *Group of Seven* (G7), the informal grouping of seven leading powers. They are the US, Japan, Germany, France, Italy, the UK and Canada. The leaders have held an annual summit since 1975, when French President Valéry Giscard d'Estaing called an informal 'fireside gathering' at Rambouillet. It has become increasingly formalised, with twice-yearly gatherings of finance ministers and central bankers and a secretariat of 'sherpas' or senior finance ministry officials. The G7 is increasingly joined by Russia for part of each summit, making it a G8, but there is a tokenism about this. The creation of the single currency makes it likely that the G7 will slim down to a G5 and perhaps ultimately a G3 of the US, Japan and Euroland.

The Gs tend to proliferate: none is abolished and others are brought into being. One of those which emerged during the Asian crisis was the G22, bringing other significant economies together with the G7 in order to consider reforms. It published three weighty reports on the international financial architecture in October 1998. Cynics dubbed it 'Friends of Larry' as its membership reflected the conclusions Lawrence Summers, then US Deputy Treasury Secretary before being promoted to the top job, was said to want it to reach. Its place as the broader forum for discussions of world economic and financial developments between the G7 and big emerging economies has been taken by the G20, which held its first regular meeting in December 1999.

There are other, proliferating clubs for different groups of countries. The twenty-nine richest countries belong to the *Organisation for Economic Co-operation and Development* (OECD), dating from the post-war reconstruction, which acts as both a think tank and an in-house forum for negotiation on taxation, trade and investment. *Asia-Pacific Economic Co-operation* (APEC) provides a venue for the US and Japan to engage with the increasingly important Asian economies, including China. *Mercosur* is a trade grouping of the Central and Latin American nations.

The *International Monetary Fund* is in effect the executive arm of the G7, whose members hold the most voting power on its Executive Board and informal influence. However, the IMF has its own formal authority structures which could become more important, notably its Interim Committee, a management committee with a policy role. In addition, the IMF is the forum in which developing countries engage with the developed on matters concerning the grand sweep of international economic governance. Even the G7 countries now seem aware that the Fund must allow developing countries greater say in its operations. Votes of the Executive Board are formally weighted by the size of the member economies. By convention the IMF is run by a European.

Its American-headed sister organisation, another created at Bretton Woods and formally under the UN umbrella, is the *World Bank*. The Bank is a group of several bodies which now share a focus on development and the poorer countries, although they started life with the aim of reconstructing war-torn Europe. They include: the International Bank for Reconstruction and Development, which makes 'soft' but semi-commercial loans to developing countries; the aid-based International Development Agency; and the private sector finance-oriented International Finance Corporation.

Both the IMF and the World Bank are Washington-based, and necessarily have a close relationship with the US Treasury Department, which played a leading role in crisis-resolution in the 1990s. Europe claims the other key international organisations. The oldest, the *Bank for International Settlements* (BIS) in Basle, is a bank for central banks. In 1998 some of the bigger and richer developing countries were invited to join, but it has essentially been a vehicle for the G10 countries – the G7 plus *eight* others! – as they account for the greater part of the world banking system. The BIS takes the leading role in bank supervision and regulation through its Basle Committee. The *International Organisation of Securities Commissions* (IOSCO) is the parallel body for securities markets, grouping stock exchanges and other national regulators.

Increasingly in the front line of controversy, as we have seen, is the *World Trade Organisation* (WTO), a successor to the semi-formal General Agreement on Tariffs and Trade, the body which had negotiated successive rounds of reductions in trade barriers since its enactment in 1948. The WTO, based in Geneva, is permanent, rules-based and with the legal power to be brought into trade disputes and force a resolution. The WTO is clearly becoming a forum for economic conflict between the US, Europe and Japan, and between developed and developing worlds. It is equally clearly still extremely ill equipped for resolving conflict. Not only is it under-staffed and lacking in institutional confidence, but it also operates in a political vacuum. This is certainly changing as trading rules in some of the most contentious possible areas, such as intellectual property, international investment and agriculture, come up for negotiation. One pressing issue is giving developing nations an effective voice when they lack the funds and expertise to staff permanent delegations at the WTO. Some G7 member governments are pushing for increased technical assistance of this kind for poor countries as a matter of urgency.

A handful of key individuals, some politicians, some of the heads of these big organisations and some senior officials from finance ministries and central banks, therefore effectively run the world economy. But they run it alongside the chief executives and heads of trading in the biggest investment banks and hedge funds, and the CEOs of some big multinationals. Power is dispersed fluidly, well outside the formal framework of the institutions created in the post-war settlement.

Demands for reform pre-date the Asian crisis. In 1994, the fiftieth anniversary of the IMF and World Bank prompted the creation of the 'Fifty Years is Enough' campaign by a coalition of external critics in the development NGOs. It was also an excuse for G7 leaders, at their summit in Halifax, Nova Scotia, to reassess the international institutions. Nothing obvious came of either drive. However, James Wolfensohn, the charismatic head of the World Bank, did embark on a programme of internal refocusing. The Bank has concentrated more than before on poverty reduction and social programmes, less on its conventional loans for big projects like dams and roads.

It was the rolling crisis of the second half of the 1990s that brought about the most serious reassessment of the existing international architecture since its construction more than half a century ago. But although the plumbing has been improved and some faulty sockets rewired – to stretch the metaphor – the original building is still standing, with just the odd lick of fresh paint and a few running repairs, in an entirely changed global economic landscape.

What went wrong?

The IMF devoted tens of billions of dollars to its efforts to stabilise the private financial markets from the Mexican crisis in December 1994 onwards. While the US Treasury devoted some of its own resources to the Mexican rescue, the IMF – whose own funds are provided by all its shareholders including the US – financed subsequent bail-outs. Each multi-billion dollar programme depended on the agreement of the government concerned to a package of economic reforms and policies acceptable to the Fund.

A classic IMF economic programme always rests on a foundation of macroeconomic orthodoxy. It advises governments to reduce their budget deficits, often requires tight monetary policy in order to reduce inflation, tends to favour privatisation of state-owned industry and deregulation in those countries that have not embraced the free market. This is not a recipe for popularity at the best of times. But never has the Fund been more vigorously criticised for its orthodoxy than in the aftermath of the Asian crisis. What's more, some of its most vigorous critics were American academics.

For example, one of the most outspoken was Jeffrey Sachs, professor of economics at Harvard University. Professor Sachs had direct experience of the limitations of free-market economics, having been one of the architects of the rapid transition to capitalism described as a 'short, sharp shock' in Eastern Europe. Outside Russia, this had been more or less a success, but the social costs and dislocations were clearly high. In Asia, the professor condemned the IMF for slavishly sticking to its original recipe when the scale of the turmoil made it inevitable that the countries affected would experience a severe recession.[1]

The IMF has mounted a vigorous defence against the charge that it set policies too tight, although admitting that with hindsight it made some mistakes. One was over-optimism about the length and depth of the recessions in each country, partly under pressure from the governments concerned to paint a rosy picture, partly so as not to alarm the fleeing investors any further. But the main defence is that interest rates had to be set high enough to stop the exchange rates of the region from nosediving so fast that there would be more capital flight out of Asian financial markets, maintaining a vicious spiral of instability. Stabilisation of the markets would be a precondition for economic recovery. Similarly, governments were allowed some leeway to expand their deficits, where these started out at relatively modest levels, but not so much that this expansion might contribute to further destabilisation.

Analysing the criticism that it had set too harsh a macroeconomic policy initially, the Fund conceded that it had been – a little – too tough, with the benefit of hindsight. But it said the prescriptions had been adjusted quickly when the depth of the downturns became apparent. The self-assessment published in September 1999 concluded: 'The initial priorities in dealing with the crisis were to stabilize the financial system and restore confidence in economic management. Forceful measures were needed to stop bank runs, protect the payments system, limit central bank liquidity support, minimize disruptions to credit flow, maintain monetary control and stem capital outflows.'[2] In short, it was a financial crisis whose speedy resolution demanded the restoration of financial confidence.

Certainly, this is plausible. The South Korean economy would not be in a better state today if the won had fallen further faster and government policies had not been vigilant against rapid inflation. On the contrary, what is striking about the Asian crisis, and the Mexican crisis before it, is the speed of recovery in countries which did swallow the bitter IMF medicine. The Latin American experience after the 1980s debt crisis has left very clear the devastating economic, social and political costs of hyperinflation and a loss of financial confidence. What is perhaps most interesting about the IMF defence, though, is its acknowledgement that real economic conditions were hostage to the episode of financial market instability.

A second criticism, expressed with less antagonism but actually more fundamental in the light of this, came from MIT's Paul Krugman. He suggested that the behaviour of the international capital markets had clearly been pathological – there was no way the plummeting currencies and stockmarkets could be behaving rationally, he argued. Country X could not be worth so many billions one day and the same amount less 40 per cent a week later, no matter what underlying problems it had. That meant there was a good case for reintroducing controls on short-term capital flows.

Krugman published a controversial article in the summer of 1998, mid-crisis, arguing in favour of exchange controls as a 'temporary curfew'.[3] Unknown to him, Malaysia was on the point of announcing exchange restrictions, and he was an unwilling hero to the government. Like Joseph Stiglitz, chief economist at the World Bank, Krugman liked the look of the Chilean experiment requiring inward investors to deposit for the first year a certain proportion of any funds they wanted to bring into the country. While this might seem a perfectly reasonable proposition to a non-economist, it is somewhat heretical within the profession. The intellectual dominance of *laissez-faire* philosophy in economics means few of its most prominent academics make a serious case for any kind of government intervention in the market. And the IMF had been lobbying successfully for some years to get member governments to agree to a change in its Articles making capital liberalisation a condition for membership. That move is now on ice.

A year later Krugman concluded the evidence was somewhat mixed. 'While Malaysia's recovery has proved the hysterical opponents of capital controls wrong, it has not exactly proved the proponents right. For there is a recovery in progress throughout Asia. South Korea, which did not impose controls . . . has bounced back with stunning speed.'[4]

At the annual meetings of the Fund and the World Bank in Washington in September 1998, just after Russia's devaluation of the rouble and partial default on its foreign debt had ratcheted up the crisis that started in Thailand just over a year earlier, there was a clear sense of crisis. President Clinton and Tony Blair described it as the worst crisis to affect the world financial system in fifty years, and announced urgent reforms of the international 'financial architecture'. Committees were set up to report on possible reforms. The IMF and World Bank set up assessments of their reactions to the crisis. Academics started to produce vast amounts of working papers and newspaper articles proposing reforms. In fact, over a year and a half on, at the time of writing, it is clear there has almost been too much thinking. There are too many specific proposals and not remotely enough consensus about the underlying principles for reform. As a result, very little has happened. The biggest crisis for half a century was not big enough to budge everybody involved to agree to radical reform.

There have, however, been modest reforms, which will help. These are directed towards prevention of future crises. The least exciting but most important is a new emphasis on what is known as 'surveillance' or 'transparency' in the jargon of international financial officials. Countries are urged to produce economic and banking statistics of higher quality and greater honesty and to publish them more often. The IMF publishes on the Internet what is available. It is encouraging member governments to allow it to publish, too, its annual economics assessments of their policies. Some are more reluctant than others to agree to this. This reluctance explains why, though the Fund's economists were well aware in 1996 and early 1997 that a problem was brewing in Asia, they could not say so in public.

Greater transparency is also being urged on the banks and corporations in emerging markets. There is growing pressure for any of these that want to attract international investment or borrow money in the international markets to adhere as much as possible to US accounting standards rather than just local standards. While US rules for reporting corporate finance might not be the most appropriate for many companies in developing countries, they would be an improvement compared with the lax standards that apply in some cases. Many emerging market banks and corporations did simply pull the wool over the eyes of outside investors in a manifestation of what has become know as 'crony capitalism'. Only the core of shareholders in the know, sometimes relations or supporters of ruling families, sometimes close-knit business oligarchies, were aware of the extent of indebtedness or the size of the companies' reserves. Adherence to extremely tough international accountancy standards would have made it harder to get away with this while seeking investment funds.

Lawrence Summers has said: 'For the American capital markets, the most important single innovation was the idea of generally accepted accounting principles.' They have, he argues, 'the potential to bring about far reaching cultural change.'[5]

This criticism of a double financial standard applies, too, to some western countries. Continental Europe has long practised its own version of crony capitalism. German and French banks are long-standing shareholders in corporations whose executives went to the same universities. Any European company wanting to raise capital on the US stockmarket has had to make big changes in its financial reporting to be able to go ahead. While the US accountancy rules are not ideal, they are just about the world's most stringent in their demands for the provision of information to investors.

Also in the wake of the crisis, the Bank for International Settlements has published proposals for more stringent reserve requirements for banks. These will replace the Basle Accord, which stipulated that banks had to hold reserves in certain types of asset worth at least 8 per cent of the value of their lending, weighted for risk, and at least 4 per cent had to take the form of their own share capital. Perversely, the Accord counted long-term loans as riskier than short-term loans, encouraging international banks to opt for the hot-money short-term lending that turned tumult in Asian financial markets into an Asian crisis and then a global crisis. Not only did some Asian banks struggle to satisfy the minimum Basle standard, but conservative bankers had always thought it was too low anyway. By contrast, in the raw capitalist days of the late nineteenth century, banks had 40 or 50 per cent reserve ratios. The combination of better risk management techniques amongst bankers and publicly funded deposit insurance for small depositors justifies a lower ratio, but recent experience suggests it had fallen too low.

The new Basle Accord could reduce the reserve requirement for a few big international banks which can convince their supervisors they have assessed correctly the risks they face of loans going bad or investments flopping. But most will end up holding more reserves. That will make them correspondingly less able to lend more money without adding more reserves. It will apply the brakes on the growth of lending, especially of riskier varieties such as loans for property, many of which in South East Asia went belly up as the crisis burst their mid-1990s property boom.

A further measure to improve financial stability was the creation of the Financial Stability Forum, a gathering of banking and finance department officials that met for the first time in March 1999, under the auspices of the IMF. This new committee in the panoply of international finan-
cial organisations is designed to improve co-ordination amongst national regulators of the financial markets. While the markets themselves have become more or less seamless, operating with ease across national boundaries, the structures of regulation have remained bounded. Past efforts to co-ordinate always fell victim to disputes over who should be in charge – not only did the US want an American regulator to take the lead, which other developed countries refused to accept as a basic principle, but the different US bodies could not agree amongst themselves which it should be. The urgency of the need has now brought some measure of co-operation over financial supervision. It remains to be seen, however, how much difference the new forum can make in conditions of turmoil. And that will be hard to assess, given that emergency financial discussions necessarily take place in secret, for speed, and to prevent panic.

Nevertheless, more co-operation between national regulators – even if it never amounts to more than exchanging information – must be a help in terms of placing restrictions on the excesses of international banks and invest-

ment funds. Co-operation between national regulators has
been inadequate – to give one example, no supervisory
bodies outside Japan had any idea of the scale of its
banking crisis until it was well under way. National pride
is at stake – many countries regard banks as national
champions. There are also the turf wars between regulators, which have led to a plethora of committees for this
and that, a classic bureaucratic response to a failure to
agree. Perhaps the new *über*-committee will improve this
a little.

The remaining measures so far adopted in response to
the crisis take the form of IMF-drafted codes of conduct
for governments, companies and social partners. There
are codes for the transparency and stability of national
fiscal and monetary policy; for the targeting of social
policies towards poverty reduction and extended opportunities for citizens; and for corporate governance that
takes account of the interests of a wide range of stakeholders, including employees. Not surprisingly, the draft
codes, which have to gain acceptance across the Fund's
membership, tend towards the bland. Even so, they
embed a rhetoric of openness, opportunity and fairness in
the IMF's programmes. This, too, can be no bad thing.

Other proposals for reform, even the relatively uncontroversial, have run into the sands of international
bureaucracy and diplomacy. For example, there was widespread agreement that in future the IMF's resources
should not simply bail private investors out of their mistakes. During the Asian crisis, the IMF's billions were
used by Asian governments to funnel to their banks to
repay debts to foreign lenders so that the panic-stricken
capital flight would stop and the exchange rate stabilise.
While foreign investors in shares lost money as the stockmarkets fell, and all lost on the foreign exchanges because
the local currency was worth so much less in dollars or

pounds, many overseas investors did not make nearly the losses that would have been a true reflection of their investment decision. Rudiger Dornbusch, the MIT economist, joked that the IMF had changed its phone number to '1-800-BAILOUT'.

The western governments calling the shots at the IMF therefore found it easy to agree the private sector would have to make a bigger contribution in future to crisis resolution. But the US and UK governments could not agree on the exact shape this should take – should it be set out in new regulations in the international bond market (the UK view), or should it be *ad hoc*, determined episode by episode with the major banks involved (the US view)? Until this question is resolved, it will be neither.

The hunt for other proposals

The list of failures to alter the international financial architecture, or even the plumbing, is longer yet. Several proposals seriously debated in the immediate aftermath of the Asian crisis have fallen by the wayside. Notable amongst them were suggested alterations to the role and structure of the International Monetary Fund itself. For example, one European-led proposal concerned the IMF's Interim Committee, originally set up to explore changes to the Fund's role in the aftermath of the 1973 break-up of the Bretton Woods fixed exchange rate system. This bit of mid-1970s architecture has taken a sort of strategic overview of the IMF ever since, but with little power. Although intermittently influential, decisions have continued to reside with the official delegates who exercise governments' votes on the IMF's Executive Board. The proposal to enhance the political role of the Interim Committee came to nothing, however. While the IMF's management would not have welcomed an additional set of political taskmasters, a slightly beefed-up Interim Committee would probably have made little difference to its operations. What it could have done, however, would have been to give the important developing nations a voice in the corridors of the Fund. As things stand, they have scant influence on the IMF, dealing with its officials as clients rather than as the shareholders or stakeholders they are supposed to be. So although the exact role of another committee sounds a minor matter, it actually goes to the heart of the problem with the IMF.

This failure to progress is therefore more serious than the much more high-profile question of whether the IMF ought to act as a 'lender of last resort'. Any national central bank plays this role. If the banking system looks to be threatened when a financial institution goes bankrupt or there is any sign of panic amongst depositors wanting to withdraw their money in a run on the banks, the central bank can step in to lend funds to any part of the system that needs it. It guarantees that the money will be there for any bank that is solvent but short of cash due to the panic. The rest of the system is isolated from the failing banks. Many bank supervisors also run deposit insurance schemes that guarantee depositors will get at least some proportion of their money back when a bank fails, and that, too, helps confine the extent of any problem.

The proposal was therefore that the IMF should take on this role on an international scale in order to prevent 'contagion' whereby, say, bank failures in Thailand would knock on to South Korean banks even when the latter were short of liquid funds – ready cash to pay out to panicking depositors and foreign lenders – but basically solvent. This question of the need for an international lender of last resort exercised commentators a great deal during the Asian crisis. In particular, pundits worried about whether giving the IMF such a role would create a 'moral hazard' problem whereby the existence of such a safety net would encourage countries to borrow excessively in the international markets knowing that there was a bailout mechanism.

However, the proposal that the IMF should become a lender of last resort was always purely academic for it is not a bank with a huge pile of its own reserves. Any national central bank has far bigger reserves relative to the size of its economy than the IMF relative to the size of the world economy. The Fund's so-called 'quota increases', whereby member countries chip in more to its reserves, have lagged far behind world economic growth – since the quota increase in 1983, they have risen by 50 per cent, whereas in the same period the world economy has roughly doubled in size and the flow of funds across international boundaries has increased by vastly more. There has never been any political appetite to create an IMF big enough to act as a world central bank. Instead, the efforts have focused on increasing the amounts it would be able to lend to countries in trouble in future. In essence, the IMF has been given a bigger overdraft facility with its rich member governments in order to increase the size of the overdrafts it can make available to countries in trouble in future crises.

An alternative approach to increasing the scale of the IMF is to shrink – or at least limit the growth or tame in some way – the international capital markets. And this was the tack taken in other sorts of proposal. One, which for a while got much support from two G7 members, France and Germany, was for an agreement on target exchange rate zones, especially between the dollar, yen and euro, the world's three main reserve currencies. The most heavily traded on the foreign exchanges, each tends to send lesser currencies bobbing up and down whenever it moves dramatically against one of the others. This is particularly true of the dollar: some emerging market currencies are actually pegged to it. Indeed, that was part of Thailand's problem in the first place. It clung to a dollar peg despite inflationary pressures from its expanding economy that meant a fixed nominal rate corresponded to an appreciation in real terms. Its exchange rate became unsustainably uncompetitive. Increasing speculation eventually forced the Thai government to give up the dollar peg, triggering the whole rolling crisis.

Intellectual fashions swing between freely floating exchange rates and fixed exchange rates, and the episode has swung them against floating. This explains why the idea of target zones, long advocated by US economist Fred Bergsten, found their way back to the policy agenda. The G7 has a history of stepping in to influence exchange rates when they get very far out of line with what are believed to be sensible levels, or when they are moving too quickly. However, the US and UK governments have for a couple of decades opposed intervention in the currency markets if it is an attempt to buck the market rather than nudge it in the direction it is likely to go anyway. The UK's disastrous experience of being forced out of the European Exchange Rate Mechanism in September 1992, after an uncharacteristic period of targeting an exchange rate level, only reinforced this earlier tendency. The idea of bands of fluctuation between G7 currencies therefore proved short-lived.

Indeed, Robert Rubin, then US Treasury Secretary, made it very clear in a speech in April 1999 that emerging economies should be discouraged from linking their currencies to the dollar or another major currency. Rather than seeing floating rates or fixed rates as two alternatives, the policy community now favours either a freely floating currency or an irrevocably fixed currency, but nothing in

between. It is the hazy area in between that allows speculators to play on uncertainty. Thus Europe's Monetary
Union is a credible and permanent fixing of exchange
rates between its members. 'Dollarisation' (or 'euroisa-
tion, for Eastern Europe) is another, whereby a smaller
economy exchanges all of its own currency for US dollars
(or euros). It eliminates exchange rate uncertainty at the
price of handing over control of interest rates and the
money supply to the US Federal Reserve (or European
Central Bank). Argentina has seriously considered this in
place of its existing currency board. Although a currency
board also links local currency permanently to the dollar,
those that exist in Argentina and Hong Kong have been
vulnerable to speculation during the crisis that the link
might not prove irrevocable

With the consensus thus crystallising that exchange rate
regimes must be either fully fixed or fully flexible, the idea
of target zones fell by the wayside. The resignation of their
main G7 proponent, Oskar Lafontaine, as Germany's
finance minister in March 1999 dealt the proposal a fatal
political blow.

Interventionist proposals

A second proposal, referred to above, was the introduction
of the 'Tobin tax', a tax on foreign exchange transactions.
A third was the reintroduction of capital controls, the re-
regulation of the currency markets.

The Tobin tax, named after its original proposer, the
Nobel Laureate James Tobin, would skim something like
0.5 per cent or 1 per cent off the nominal value of
currency trades. Much loved by the left, it would be a
nonsense in practice, and has never been considered
seriously in policy circles. One sort of objection concerns

the practicalities. Which governments would impose the tax on a two-sided transaction? If mainly the US and UK, because the international banks operate out of the big money centres, would they have to share the revenues with other countries? How could the tax regulations be drawn up so that they could not be evaded easily through derivatives transactions? For if a straight exchange of currencies were taxed, it would be as easy as anything to do the same thing through a swap. Once you start trying to take account of all the possible evasions, a Tobin tax would quickly become impossible to administer. While governments did indeed manage to control foreign exchange transactions up to about 1980, that was before derivatives had been devised, and also in the days when all economies were more centrally directed and corporatist than they are now.

More fundamentally, the Tobin tax is just misconceived. At the proposed levels it would make scarcely any difference to the amount of currency trades. Exchanging dollars into bahts already involves very high transactions costs – high brokerage fees in Bangkok, for example. And these would be dwarfed either by the desire to invest in the Thai market or by the profit margin the speculator expected to make. If a 'tax' of 10–30 per cent did not deter the transaction, neither would a 1 per cent Tobin tax.

The alternative would be the restoration of exchange restrictions, which have been progressively lifted over the past twenty years. Some commentators regard the wartime and post-war period of exchange controls as a norm to which the world should seek to return. Capital controls were, as Keynes made clear, a way of avoiding the 'trilemma' of economic policy in an open economy. A government has two weapons, monetary and fiscal policy, to hit three targets: domestic growth, a balance of payments that balances, and a stable exchange rate. It can never achieve all three at once, and will lurch from problem to problem. Controls introduce a third weapon.

And certainly since the Asian crisis the IMF and G7 policy-makers have accepted that emerging markets should not be forced or encouraged to lift all their remaining capital controls in a hurry. They do offer a buffer for small economies opening up to the world, even if mainly because not much finance flows into such countries anyway. As was noted above, Malaysia temporarily introduced restrictions on the ability of investors to take money out of the country. This stabilised the exchange rate, but the penalty was that foreign investors stopped putting any money in. There has been more interest in Chile's requirement for investors to deposit a proportion of their funds for a year, as a means of discouraging short-term speculative flows. This indeed worked well until the crisis. Chile was little affected by the waves of financial turbulence. However, it had to reduce the reserve requirement in April 1998 and suspend it in September that year, again because foreign investment had dried up. The problem for developing countries is that they cannot set the terms if they want to participate in the international capital markets. And despite the problems, most do still want access to the entire global pool of funds to finance development. There is no alternative to playing by the rules of the game.

Indeed, the most striking absence in all of the post-crisis debate has been the lack of serious proposals about changing the ground rules. International financial architecture is a misleading metaphor. It suggests what is at stake is a question of technical fixes, when the problem is fundamentally political.

Failure to tackle the big issues

One issue unaddressed by the specifics of the post-crisis fixes is the distribution of power between national governments and international bodies. For nowhere is there a clearer example of the limits the forces of globalisation place on governments than in the financial markets. The markets, which means big commercial and investment banks, pension and insurance funds, hedge funds, and so on, are inherently cross-border. Although each of these financial institutions has a home country, reporting to a home regulator, they operate in many countries. Many of the hedge funds, over which hangs the charge of causing speculative mayhem, are based in light-regulation tax havens. A study by the US Congress in the wake of the near-collapse of Long Term Capital Management, one of the biggest and best-known of the lot, found that there was essentially nothing the US government could do to regulate these investment funds more tightly.

It is precisely this sort of realisation that lies behind calls for new or stronger international organisations, in order to govern the international banks and investment funds. Thus the proposal that the IMF should act as a lender of last resort. Similarly, John Eatwell, a Cambridge economist close to Tony Blair, proposed a new global financial authority to act as a supervisor of the global market.[6]

In the same vein, the heart of the prominent critique of global markets published by George Soros in late 1998 was that national political systems cannot cope with global financial markets.[7] The markets have become, in his metaphor, a 'wrecking ball' swinging to and fro across the world destroying whatever gets into their path. He believes that free markets must be retained for their efficiency, but must be controlled by supra-national bodies.

The real trouble with demands for more intervention by international organisations or new bodies to control the markets, however, is their failure to address the politics of such supra-national policies. After all, there is hardly convincing evidence that the existing corps of technocrats can do the job when the politics is left out of it.

International organisations are inter-governmental organisations, prone to the usual intricacies of diplomacy and conflicts of national interest. It is hardly as if the transnational agencies that exist are famed for their speed, efficiency or even honesty. On the contrary, all are criticised for being nothing more than talking shops, and extravagant ones at that with their window dressing of diplomatic missions and cocktail parties. There is nothing more certain to bring disrepute on an international economic agency supposed to be reducing poverty or eliminating financial crises than one ill-judged display of luxury.

More to the point, experience suggests the world is far from any form of international economic governance in the sense of a body with the genuine authority to set regulations or otherwise intervene in international markets. The World Trade Organisation comes closest, with its legalistic, rule-based powers to apply sanctions to national governments. It is no coincidence that it is so controversial, the forum for conflict between national governments. In general, global powers of governance rest on international treaties that cede areas of national sovereignty – and the IMF is one of the few organisations to have an international treaty base, which is what makes it the key forum for discussing improvements.

A new organisation, a global regulator of the financial markets, would need a new world-wide treaty. Building such institutions is not easy. The creation of the Bretton

Woods institutions at the tail-end of the Second World War occurred in exceptional circumstances, when there was a blank sheet of paper, a clear political determination and vision about what shape the new international governance should take. What's more, the architects of Bretton Woods had fresh memories of the Great Depression and its terrible social and political consequences. Yet that kind of catastrophic breakdown has been rare in the history of capitalism – it might well be crisis-prone, but many of the crises turn out to be not so bad after all.

So it is with the Asian crisis, at least for the developed economies only indirectly affected by it. The same political impetus for radical reform simply does not exist now – the willingness to contemplate the radical is in proportion to the scale of the crisis, and the Asian crisis was not enough to drive the world powers to consider starting over. Perhaps more to the point, most of the episodes of financial crisis hit second-class economies, not first-class ones. The latter have financial systems with enough liquidity and enough institutional resilience to steer a course through the turmoil. It was not until a year on, when the crisis threatened to spill over into US and European financial markets, that the leading powers even contemplated far-reaching reforms. The enthusiasm abated as rapidly as the financial turbulence. While international treaties are becoming steadily more extensive and important as the process of globalisation continues, we are a long way from international government. Meanwhile, international government is a cumbersome and unsatisfactory alternative in practice.

In theory too. Good governance must involve, amongst other things, a minimum degree of legitimacy. There is little enough of this in existing international organisations. All are at best jargon-ridden fora for technocrats and diplomats. At worst they are secretive and anti-democratic. They have made real progress on improving the management of the world's financial markets post-crisis – but, as one senior UK official put it: 'The international community operates in an extremely indeterminate way.' It is hard to be sure exactly what decisions are reached and when. The IMF is not guilty on many charges, but it is obsessed with secrecy and utterly lacking in accountability or political legitimacy. Only now that its own rhetoric places so much emphasis on transparency – and in the wake of its biggest internal as well as external crisis for a generation – is it slowly starting to open up. Its sister organisation, the World Bank, is just a bit further ahead, having redefined its mission as centred on poverty reduction and the world's poor. But it has taken decades of lobbying from environmental and aid groups to get the World Bank to accept that poor people matter in economic development.

The role of the IMF in particular is still in the process of evolution, and a secretive and highly politicised process it is. The external manifestation was the embarrassingly inept international horse-trading over the choice of a successor to Michel Camdessus as the Fund's managing director. Horst Köhler, the German bureaucrat eventually named as head of the IMF, was not even the first choice of his own government. The shambolic procedure fell victim to the determination of the US Treasury to ensure the candidate, although required by convention to be European, would go along with US policy requirements. In particular, the American administration wanted to ensure the IMF would concentrate on its 'core' activity of short-term lending to correct macroeconomic problems.

Critics argue that narrowing the IMF's remit will ensure the Fund is increasingly an instrument of US foreign policy. Its loans to Russia have been particularly heavily criticised for this very reason. One of the most thoughtful assessments of IMF activities, from a bipartisan committee of American experts headed by Carnegie Mellon economics professor Allan Meltzer,[8] claims that this politicisation is the fundamental problem. Although its specific proposals also call for a more tightly focused Fund, arguing that all long-term development lending should be left to the World Bank, the political nature of the institution is at the heart of its analysis. Professor Meltzer argues that the IMF will remain a sick institution until the internal balance of power starts to tilt away from the US and the rest of the G7 and towards the middle ranks of industrialising countries. Yet without a broad political consensus even within policy-making circles in the G7 countries on the direction for reform, change will continue to take shape behind closed doors in Washington.

The failings of existing and, indeed, potential official international organisations mean that in effect the US, the world's hegemonic economic power, acts as the only force of governance in the world economy. To the extent that global financial markets are regulated, it happens in New York. The US Treasury has a decisive influence over the World Bank and IMF, both based in Washington. Contrary to the gut reaction of many critics, the US government agencies do a pretty good job, but of course they do it with US interests at heart.

Posing formal international institutions as the only alternative form of world economic governance to US domination misses an important trick. It overlooks the importance of international civil society and the political economy of international finance.

Alternative approaches to reform

This inclusion of politics in international economic governance will have to be more than the kind of anti-globalisation protests we are increasingly witnessing, the radical romantic backlash that has focused on the MAI and the WTO. Environmental activists lobbing bottles at the police or animal rights activists setting fire to the odd truck do not amount to a political movement. A better model is the Jubilee 2000 coalition of aid agencies, churches and other non-governmental organisations campaigning for G7 governments to wipe clean the slate on third world debt for the new millennium. Jubilee 2000 will not achieve its full aims, but it has made a big difference, shifting the international financial agenda and making a material difference to the lives of some of the world's very poorest people.

The forty or so poorest countries owed, by 1999, some $300bn in official international debt – that is, owed to institutions such as the World Bank and IMF or the Inter-American Development Bank. During the 1990s it became clear to even the most orthodox financiers that the debt burden was unsustainable. These poor economies grew so little that they did not generate enough money to pay the debt interest, so the overhang grew ever bigger. An initial 'Highly Indebted Poor Countries' or HIPC initiative was drafted by the IMF, the aim being to write off enough of the debt and accumulated interest to get the countries to a sustainable position where they could repay their remaining debts and expand their economies. To qualify, a country had to have stuck to an IMF programme of economic reform and satisfy certain threshold criteria such as the ratio of debt interest payments to export earnings. Too high, and it would qualify for a partial write-off.

This was the situation after an initial bout of lobbying by the aid organisations and strong political pressure within the G7 from the UK (under both Conservative and Labour chancellors) and Canada. The total cost to the lenders of the planned debt relief was initially put at $7bn, a truly miserly amount of money made the more meagre when you remember it was to be split forty ways.

When it looked as though this would be the only pitiful fruit of the long and hard-fought process of campaigning for debt relief, Jubilee 2000 and other non-governmental organisations stepped up into a higher gear with their fresh call for a completely clean slate on third world debt. A popular campaign, cleverly conducted and drawing in stars from the entertainment world, made it a high-profile issue in a majority of the G7 countries. Thousands of British people sent postcards in the spring of 1999 to their own chancellor, congratulating him on persuading some G7 governments to finance more generous debt relief for highly indebted poor countries, and to the German finance ministry, demanding that it should stop blocking the improved programme. A movement from within civil society eventually achieved $100bn-worth of debt relief (although it would cost the lenders much less) in a much better programme.

The call for a full debt write-off was always in one way wrong-headed. Every government in the world has an international debt, and what matters is that it should not be too big relative to the size of the economy. To write off all of the debt owed by countries like Mozambique and Nicaragua would leave the IMF and World Bank with no funds left for their aid programmes in other desperately poor countries like Bangladesh, which happened not to have incurred big overseas debts. Yet the extreme demand – write off all the debt of all developing countries – was politically sensible, a highly moral but also highly simple aim that bounced the G7 governments into something very much more generous than they had originally envisaged. As Jubilee 2000 pointed out at a crucial stage in the debate within the G7, Germany had had its debts, incurred by the Nazi government, forgiven in the 1951 London Agreement, allowing the country to go on to its post-war economic miracle with a completely fresh start. When the IMF and World Bank had lent billions to unpalatable dictators like Presidents Mobuto or Marcos, it is a powerful argument.

For the foreseeable future the politics of the international economy will take this shape. Grassroots campaigns, the agglomeration described by Andrew Marr as the 'alternative opposition',[9] will confront the powers of the international banks and multinational corporations better than any existing or new international organisations. They will also confront the priorities and philosophy of those international organisations, bringing real political engagement to an arena so far dominated by technocrats and G7 or at least US interests. The debt relief campaign is only one example. An earlier campaign by environmentalists in the 1980s fundamentally – although slowly – shifted the World Bank's approach to the environment, marking the beginning of the end for the ecologically damaging big infrastructure projects the Bank had always liked to finance. It also opened the way for the World Bank to focus on reducing poverty rather than the more abstract idea of 'economic development', so open to technocratic interpretation.

More recently, NGOs have led a campaign for the improvement of conditions in third world factories either run by multinationals or given contracts by them. This has also been too simplistic in its analysis. For instance, multinationals are usually better employers than local companies. Some of the most totemic US multinationals, such as Disney and Nike Mattel, have been given a seal of approval for their world-wide employment standards by no less politically correct an authority than the United Nations Development Programme.[10] The arrival of these corporations in a country signals the start of an increase in living standards, not only because they create jobs but also because they start bidding up local wage rates. They are also just about the only channel through which developing economies get access to new technologies. Japan and, to some extent, South Korea are exceptions in having got to the frontier of technology through the efforts of home-grown companies rather than technology transfer by multinationals.

More fundamentally, first world conditions cannot be re-created in a third world economy. If it were easy, there would no longer be a third world – and, contrary to the beliefs of many in the alternative opposition movement, there is no explicit US/IMF/banking conspiracy to keep the poor that way. There are no shortcuts for many parts of the growth process. Education and public health, for example. Labour is cheap in developing countries because the workforce is far less productive than its western counterparts, and that is why only unskilled tasks are sourced from them. Such countries need to get a start on the growth to make the social and physical investments to help them on to further development.

For this reason the campaign to prevent poor workers from exploitation by multinationals needs to be treated with caution. Many politicians and intellectuals in developing countries regard this as a backdoor method of raising barriers to trade – and, indeed, American and French unions support the campaign in order to keep some cheap imports out and to protect their own members' jobs. This verges on the outright immoral. Cheap exports to our markets are the one sure, tried and tested route to increased prosperity outside the western world.

Even so, it is encouraging that the anti-multinationals campaigns exist. They are a sign of increasingly pragmatic engagement in the process of globalisation in the financial markets and world economy generally. This is certainly better than the romantic rejection that characterised initial opposition. It also offers greater hope for actually shaping that process. The politics of the globalised economy will be characterised not by bigger or better inter-governmental institutions but by a far more flexible and informal organisational network. It will incorporate not only the national governments and international bureaucracies that already exist, but also institutions of civil society. Some non-governmental organisations are shaping up for a leading role in this, but NGOs can also form shifting political networks across borders, often connected by the Internet to grassroots movements. They are enabled by technology in a way that has become possible only in the past few years. They are more agile and faster-acting in the face of events than are formal power structures. What they lack is a determination to go beyond pure opposition.

5

The New 'New Economy'

There are at present two grand narratives concerning the world economy. So far this book has dealt with one of them: globalisation, and, more specifically, its implications for the institutions governing the world economy. The other is what has come to be known as the 'new economy' story. It addresses the technology-triggered boom that the US economy has enjoyed in recent years even as the most important emerging economies in Asia suffered the worst financial crisis the world had seen for half a century. The two narratives are linked, and looking at the nature of those links sheds light on how the world economy is taking shape at the start of the twenty-first century.

There is a causal link between them. It lies in the advances in information technology, telecommunications and also biotechnology, combined with the post-Cold War political trend towards deregulation and free markets. On the one hand these drove forward the globalisation of financial markets and boosted trade and investment flows. On the other, they laid the ground for the development of a massively entrepreneurial new industry in the US, the fall in unemployment to thirty-year lows and a record US economic expansion.

In turn, the very success of the American economy – which shrugged off, thanks to the intervention of the

Federal Reserve, the potential impact of the crisis on the domestic financial system – laid the foundations for the American dominance of the global landscape. Whatever its many problems, and however much others might dislike the US model, no other model appeared to be functional. The European model could not generate jobs and lacked the dynamism that would lay the foundations of continuing economic success in future. And the Asian model, in which many commentators had placed such high hopes as an alternative to the brutalities of 'Anglo-Saxon' capitalism, had been pretty comprehensively damaged by the 1997–8 crisis.

That crisis generated, as we have seen, two types of reaction, which could be labelled 'triumphalism' and 'opposition', each with their partisans.

Good examples of the former can be found often in places like the editorial page of the *Wall Street Journal*. For instance, one such editorial, headlined 'The "Global" World is Anglo-Saxon', argued that the post-war corporatist economic model centred on the interests of manufacturers and exporters, in Germany and Japan as well as many developing countries, was imploding. Its author, David Roche, wrote: 'The economic model that will be substituted for the post-war reconstruction one will be the Anglo-Saxon market-driven model with local characteristics.' This would boost efficiency and productivity enormously through a global supply-side revolution. It would sever the nexus of links between governments and national corporations in favour of a global web of market relationships, he went on.[1]

At the opposite extreme is the movement coalescing around opposition to the MAI, the WTO, the IMF and other international financial acronyms. One journalist, Bruce Shapiro, in the on-line *Salon Magazine*, labelled the riots in Seattle the 'Gdansk of Globalisation' in a parallel with the 1980s Polish opposition movement which brought together traditional unions and radicals in opposition to an oppressive hierarchy.

> In Seattle, long-simmering cultures of opposition emerged with an articulate common challenge to the worldwide corporate agenda. The century's-end convergence of mass protest and collapsed negotiations in the world capital of the information-age economy mark the end of a 20-year infatuation with corporate deregulation, a cult of the global marketplace that began under President Reagan and finally collided head-on with reality in the streets of Seattle and the conference rooms of the WTO.[2]

Both postures suffer, however, from taking globalisation as an inevitable, inexorable process that is 'out there' to be reacted to, embraced or opposed. Both suffer from a type of economic determinism. Doreen Massey challenges this deterministic view, spelling out the way the conceptualisation of the modern nation state, including its specific relation to space, reflected particular power structures. 'One of the effects of modernity was the establishment of a particular power/knowledge relation which was mirrored in a geography which was also a geography of power (the colonial powers/the colonised spaces).' Now, she argues, there is a grand narrative of economic globalisation which sees the world of the future as an unbounded trading space. 'World economic leaders gather (in Washington, Paris or Davos) to congratulate themselves upon, and to flaunt and reinforce their powerfulness, a powerfulness which consists in insisting that they (we) are powerless – in the face of globalising market forces there is absolutely nothing that can be done.'[3]

But to speak of globalisation in general is automatically to give it a false air of inevitability. There is only globalisation in its specifics. Even if there is an inevitability, driven by technology, in the growing interconnectedness of different places and people, the nature and terms of the connections are open to challenge. Massey writes: 'If the world is becoming more interconnected then it is doing so and must do so in the context of particular power relations, and governed by particular political trajectories.'[4]

The international financial and economic crisis of 1997–8 highlights the limitations and strengths of the orthodox version of globalisation, the one which could be characterised as a right-wing or neo-liberal version. If it were absolutely right, there should not have been a crisis. If it were absolutely wrong, there could not have been such a rapid recovery from crisis. The international community has muddled through without sacrificing the vision of free market globalisation.

Certainly, the 'New Economy' success of the US in generating rapid growth, falling unemployment, low inflation and rising living standards must hold lessons for other countries – just as its failures, like the lack of health care for 40 million citizens or the high prison population, mean it should learn lessons from elsewhere.

The New Economy

The phrase 'New Economy' is actually used to refer to many things, from the stockmarket boom in dot.com company shares on Wall Street to the complex of economic and social changes being driven by technical developments – especially the Internet – and by the broader process of globalisation. The biggest enthusiasts argue that the door is open to an era of economic plenty, that the rules of scarcity are redundant, that a new Industrial Revolution is under way. More modestly, it is argued that, thanks to global competition, high growth will not be checked by rising inflation, allowing the return of the post-war golden era of expansionist policies and low unemployment. This calmer version has made real headway in the corridors of power, with Alan Greenspan, the Federal Reserve Board chairman, its most prominent adherent.

There is little evidence in economic statistics, at least outside the US, that the New Economy has made any difference yet to trend rates of growth or productivity increase, which is what ultimately determines the pace of improvement in living standards. The idea that there is something fundamentally new taking place has many sceptics, with the numbers on their side. However, difficult as it is to be confident about the newness of the New Economy in the absence of real evidence, it is equally hard to dismiss the notion of change. After all, the links between particular technical advances and social and economic change were equally hazy a century and a half ago.

It is now well understood that the implementation of new technologies can take decades. They have to be embedded in new investment and often require a big social reorganisation within companies and the broader economy. Certainly, for anything that involves building a network, the spread of technology can be very slow. It took fifty years between the development of the technical capacity to generate electricity and the building of the first power station in the United States (in 1882), and then another fifty years before electricity powered as much as four-fifths of American businesses and households.

In a well-known paper, the economic historian Paul David at Stanford described how it took forty years for US industry to reorganise in order to exploit efficiently the electric motor.[5] It needed more than the spread of the technology – the list of preconditions surely includes limited liability, development of the banking industry, free trade and a reliable framework of contract law and competition policy.

Arguably, it also needed the extension of primary education universally to create the industrial workforce. When it did, the world got mass production and mass consumption. The fruits of the technological revolution, however, were the assembly line and corporatism.

The necessary large-scale investment in the new information and communications technologies is actually a recent phenomenon even in the US. Businesses just weren't spending all that much of their investment budgets on new technologies until the current expansion started in 1992. Since then this investment has been growing at a double-digit annual rate. The IT share of the US economy, as estimated by the Commerce Department, almost doubled from 4.2 per cent in 1977 to 8.2 per cent in 1998. And outlays on equipment and capitalised software as a proportion of GDP climbed to the highest in post-war history in 1999. By this time, other developed countries had begun to follow suit.

New technologies perhaps only have their full economic effect when they have also achieved much of their ultimate cultural impact. Maybe there is a parallel in the railways. The railways fired the Victorian imagination in much the same way as the Internet inspires many of us. It was not until rail companies had linked up that the UK had a consistent national time. Many parts of the country, even individual towns, had their own time zones. The rail network transformed the everyday notion of time and punctuality, and made uniformity of time and ultimately factory time-keeping possible. Railways also changed people's understanding of distance. The death of distance was proclaimed a century ago. It underpinned nineteenth-century globalisation and the creation of empires. Computers have fundamentally changed the mental landscape once again. It hardly matters if the physical landscape is slow to catch up. The railways allowed humans to master distance. Computers and telecoms have made it irrelevant, which is why we see both globalisation and the renewed importance of local geography.

Every new technology has its sceptics. Harry M. Warner, founder of Warner Brothers, said in 1927: 'Who the hell wants to hear actors talk?' Some people could not imagine any use for wireless broadcasts – who would pay for messages broadcast over the ether to no-one in particular? His company, merged into the giant media conglomerate Time Warner in 1990, merged in January 2000 with America Online, the biggest of the new Internet companies. It was the biggest ever merger in corporate history, creating a corporation worth $350bn, and an apt symbol of the arrival of the Internet in mainstream business.

Other bright new ideas have failed in the past, or turned out to be pretty unexciting in the end. However, I believe that the Internet and further advances in biotechnology and nanotechnology will turn out to have a profound impact on our societies and lives. If so, there is a lot that is up for grabs. The Wall Street bubble could easily burst, making the US triumphalism look rather silly, but that will not destroy the potential for improvement in day-to-day life. It is important that the potential benefit is shared more fairly than it has been so far – both within the rich countries, and on a global basis.

The political role of the Internet

In addition to its economic impact, the Internet is facilitating the globalisation of the opposition to globalisation, or what many commentators would characterise as an emerging trans-national civil society. Rather than employing the broad definition of civil society as the entire gamut of associations that exist in the public domain but separate from the state, they tend to mean the rapidly growing number of international advocacy groups and non-governmental organisations. There are now well over 5,000 of these trans-national NGOs. These are increasingly co-operating on particular issues. Good examples are the opposition to the MAI and WTO.

The earliest example of protest organised effectively over the Internet was perhaps support for Mikhail Gorbachev during the attempted August 1991 coup against him. The leaders of the coup had seized control of radio and TV networks in the traditional way, but not the telephone network. The scientists running the fledgeling computer network provided an alternative flow of information both within the country and to the outside world. The protests against the MAI and the WTO meeting in Seattle were definitely organised in large part over the Internet, as were other events like the 18 June 1999 riot in London. The network is slowly nibbling away at censorship and repression. One group, the Global Internet Liberty Campaign, lobbies governments not to restrict access to the Net.

The UNDP has highlighted more constructive potential for the Net, noting that in 1990 most of the available data on Africa were stored and managed in the US and Europe, unavailable to African researchers. Now policymakers and academics in that continent can gain access to the information and to international expertise, subject to pretty basic problems like availability of equipment and reliability of power supply and telephone connections.

However, it would be wrong to accept at face value the claim some of these NGOs make to being, in some way, the true voice of the world's poor, or in some sense more democratic than any state-sponsored international organisations. Even in a domestic context there is growing scepticism about the strong claims some make to know public opinion better than elected governments. In the global context, claims to special legitimacy are even more problematic. In a recent article, Thomas Carothers of the Carnegie Endowment for International Peace argued:

> Most of the new transnational civil society actors are Western groups projecting themselves into developing and transitional societies. They may sometimes work in partnership with groups from those countries, but the agendas and values they pursue are usually their own. Transnational civil society is thus 'global' but very much part of the same projection of Western political and economic power that civil society activists decry in other venues.[6]

In fact, there is an urgent need to strengthen the formal institutions of international economic governance if the simplistic populism of the Web-linked opposition movement is not to derail good economic policies. Too much civil society can be a bad thing if the state is too weak to mediate democratic demands in a formal political context. At the global level, the process of globalisation has left the bodies that correspond to international state structures too weak in the face of both the increasingly organised NGOs and the increasingly powerful big corporations and banks. Although a global economic government would be both undesirable and unrealistic, the international community of governments and officials must take steps to strengthen its own influence and powers.

The economic policy demands of globalisation

The new communications technologies bringing us a hyper-global world economy are also a force for the hyper-local. One of the manifestations of this is the elevation in importance of policies and institutions which were formerly of domestic interest only. The local is global. Any aspect of a country's or company's performance can come under intense global scrutiny.

What's more, the immaturity of the international financial markets compared to the domestic markets in the most developed economies amplifies the tendency of investors to herd, for safety's sake. Virtue is extravagantly rewarded, vice punished out of all proportion. This in itself puts an additional premium on good economic policies at every level, from the broad sweep of macroeconomic policy and exchange rate management down to the details of bank regulation and accounting legislation.

In a remarkable speech given soon after he had announced his planned retirement in February 2000, Michel Camdessus, managing director of the International Monetary Fund, diagnosed a new type of crisis in the world of globalised financial markets, very different from earlier episodes, which had mainly been balance of payments crises resulting from mistakes in macroeconomic policy. Those were relatively easy to handle, or at least well understood. 'Crises of this new type explode on the open capital markets, arise from complex dysfunctions and are much less exclusively macroeconomic in nature,' he said. In Asia, for example, they laid bare 'a much more fundamental crisis in the economic management model to which the previous successes had complacently been attributed, but which was quite simply in conflict with the new demands of a globalized economy.'

He went on to argue that the ease with which crises could spread in a globalised economy 'adds a new dimension to the duty of excellence that is required of every government in the management of its economy . . . Globalisation is, in fact, a prodigious factor in accelerating and spreading the international repercussions of domestic policies – for better or for worse.' And policy-makers had in recent years come to recognise that there was a circular relationship – a vicious spiral or virtuous circle, depending on circumstances – between different aspects of policy, macroeconomic management, the soundness of the financial system, 'high-quality' growth fairly shared and poverty reduction. 'I call your attention to this circular relation: it was not seen that way some time ago. The recognition of this fact by world policymakers is a major silent breakthrough.'[7]

Another way of expressing this is to note the increased importance of 'social capital' in the globalised world economy. This is shorthand for the quality of government, of market institutions, of the legal framework, and of personal and business relations. Countries with extensive corruption, widespread Mafia activity and poorly enforced contract law have low social capital. Almost by definition, the developed economies have, in their idiosyncratic ways, high social capital.

This is too stylised a characterisation, of course. Its flaws are highlighted by the Asian crisis. Beforehand, the Asian model of capitalism was held up as an attractive and even superior alternative to conventional western capitalism, placing a stronger emphasis on stability, cohesion and continuity. Afterwards, it was reinterpreted as 'crony capitalism', corrupt, inefficient and excessively rigid.

There are elements of truth in both versions. The distinctive South East Asian version of market capitalism had obviously achieved enormous success during the mid-1970s to mid-1990s. It had delivered astoundingly rapid real growth year after year, raising living standards and creating a skilled workforce and something rapidly approaching a modern industrial economy. South Korea had indeed just joined the ranks of the OECD, the rich countries' club, when the financial crisis started. Many of the countries affected by the crisis had been running macroeconomic policies that more or less conformed to the IMF's model of orthodoxy, with low government borrowing and a trade surplus. Whatever weaknesses existed, they had not mattered for at least the previous decade.

On the other hand, the weaknesses revealed by the crisis were real too. All of the banking systems in South East Asia suffered from having lent too freely money that was unlikely ever to be repaid, perhaps because the loan was going to a member of the president's family, or to a corporation that was part of the same conglomerate and whose executives played golf together. Accountancy rules had been too relaxed, so that bankers had no knowledge of and no way of knowing what risks they were undertaking. None of the countries had created an adequate safety net insuring against unemployment, of the kind which provides an automatic social cushion and economic stability mechanism in the West. While these were faults punished disproportionately in the financial markets, they were faults nonetheless, and are now steadily being remedied.

It is the fine detail of economic policy that will increasingly help determine a country's economic performance. Macroeconomic policy problems have been solved in the sense that it is now clear, for example, after a decade or so of experimentation in the 1970s, that sustained large government budget deficits are inflationary and self-defeating in the end. Or that the longer a currency stays over-valued, the more dramatic its eventual collapse will be.

These lessons do indeed set some limits on government policy. They can even be caricatured as limits set by financial market vigilantes. But this does not change the fact that it is just bad policy for a government to spend, year after year, substantially more than it is willing to ask current or future taxpayers to fund. After all, the vigilante power of the markets arises only from the fact that governments seek to borrow huge amounts of money from them.

The emerging lessons of the 1990s concern the importance of sound microeconomic and financial policies, and also of the social underpinnings of a successful market economy. Economic success rests on a sound physical infrastructure, good regulatory and competition policies, and appropriate bankruptcy and contract law. It demands an increasingly skilled workforce. A thriving economy also requires a society whose institutions are able to handle and mediate conflicts between different social groups. And, as Amartya Sen argues, democracy is central to development, which, in his view, must be defined in terms of increasing human capabilities.[8]

These are much harder problems than the old questions of macroeconomic management. They depend far more on detail and evidence, and also on each country's past history. There are fewer big-picture solutions and actually in many areas far fewer ideological priors. This is precisely why some commentators pine for the days before policy became so dull and managerial. It is difficult to have a grand, passionate theory about accountancy standards or how to regulate the electricity industry.

This is not to say that the politics has been taken out of

economics. All policies create their own constituencies and change can be difficult. This is as true of the rich countries, with powerful industry lobbies and active consumer movements, as of the poor ones, where the top jobs in business are filled through political nepotism.

An agenda for change

One of the officials I interviewed in the course of writing this book said he had recently come to the conclusion there was now more published on the question of how to reform the world economy than a single person could read. Any author presenting a shopping list of proposals should therefore do so with the greatest hesitation. Here I offer a few in three areas of international economic governance: trade, the global financial markets, and reform of the IMF and World Bank. While not exactly modest or narrow in scope, they might be feasible and would, I believe, improve the management of the world economy – and, more important, bring some hope of achieving even the limited UN target of halving the number of people living on less than $1 a day by 2015.

The WTO is an important institution for developing countries. It is the international forum where formally their vote counts as much as America's or Europe's and where the rules treat them equally, and they should continue to try to exploit this. The single most important step would be to launch a new round of trade talks with an emphasis on market access for developing countries. This would include agreement by the US, EU and Japan to liberalise their agricultural sectors.

The WTO agenda should also include, as a high priority, technical assistance to enable developing countries to exploit fully the trading system, providing them with training and legal advice, and even a budget for their diplomatic representation. It must meet the challenges posed by new technology, reopening the TRIPs agreement and also considering the trading framework for cyber-space.

There should also be negotiations over an international framework for investment. The WTO would be the logical forum to establish ground rules for multinationals, but, given its other problems, combined with the political saliency of anything that might look like another MAI, this is perhaps not practical. However, the OECD has recently announced a new draft code of conduct for multinationals in its member countries which includes for the first time reference to minimum environmental and labour standards.

This has further hurdles before it is accepted by OECD governments. It will not apply to companies based in non-OECD countries, and (as this was written) faced a chance of being watered down so it did not apply to OECD multinationals' investments in other countries outside the club. But it does offer the prospect of a voluntary code of behaviour (rather than legally binding rules) for cross-border investment that incorporates social concerns. Indeed, it goes further than the MAI in covering action against corruption and other aspects of corporate governance. The new code ties in to the OECD's other back-stage, but extremely important, work combating tax avoidance and money-laundering. The upside of the current vogue for bashing the WTO is that other organisations have a spell out of the spotlight to get on with important reforms.

Going beyond the scope of the WTO, it would be possible to identify a huge wish-list of international reforms, from more vigorous anti-competition policy, through co-operation between national regulators, to the creation of a level regulatory playing field in industries such as telecommunications, software and biotechnology. Starting from the present position of US dominance, the rules will naturally tend to favour American companies. Preventing this pattern from intensifying will be a diplomatic challenge for other nations, as the experience of trying to agree common technical standards in television and mobile telephony, for example, already demonstrates.

In the case of the financial markets, I have argued that it is important not to see them as somehow separate and 'out there', monsters of the collective imagination. Economies get the financial markets they deserve. For all their over-reaction and instability, the markets do react to policies, not dictate them.

The Asian crisis of 1997 8, which affected four economies in South East Asia, has made a compelling case for liberalising carefully. But it has not undermined the arguments for permitting free flows of capital. The funds are value-free; it is their context that matters. There is never an issue of 'bad' flows of capital between, say, New York and Indiana, or between France and Spain. There can, however, be bad, or unsustainable, exchange rate systems or market structures or supervisory regimes.

So temporary capital controls make a sensible addition to the policy-makers' toolkit in times of financial emergency. But permanent restrictions do not, nor does a speculative tax. Neither is practicable either. Indeed, even temporary capital controls require a ban on derivatives transactions by domestic banks and will never be entirely watertight in the face of a determined flight of capital. Still, as the IMF itself has conceded, short-term controls offer a potential breathing space during a crisis. Controls also need to be as transparent and non-arbitrary as possible, to ensure they do not scare off future, welcome, overseas investment any more than necessary.

What's more, it is clearly important for emerging economies still in the process of deregulating their financial markets to do so cautiously. Banking reform and the creation of a rigorous system of financial supervision must come first, for the Asian crisis has shown how high is the price of inadequate regulation. Increased transparency and better regulation must be high on the agenda for all developing countries now. The Asian and Pacific economies that had strong regulators, alongside a tough monetary authority with a high level of foreign exchange reserves, withstood the crisis to a surprising degree. They include Hong Kong, Singapore, Taiwan, Australia and New Zealand.

Beyond the 'Washington Consensus'

The moral here is that playing a full part in the globalised economy does impose a requirement for good policies as a necessary, although not always sufficient, condition for avoiding crises. It was at a conference in 1990, sponsored by the prestigious Institute for International Economics in Washington, DC, that the term 'Washington Consensus' was coined. This was a collection of policy prescriptions for developing economies which were squarely in the tradition of orthodox economics: sound government finances, liberalisation of trade and investment, privatisation, deregulation, and so on.

It was a received wisdom that was probably never widely enough shared to deserve the term 'consensus', even though most governments in most parts of the world put its precepts into practice throughout the 1990s. But since the global financial crisis, the Washington Consensus has looked a bit threadbare. The afflicted Tigers of South East Asia had embraced it wholeheartedly and yet many of them still plunged into turmoil.

The new consensus is that the standard policy recommendations were not wrong, just incomplete. Critics will say this is a bid by one of the Big Brother institutions of the world economy to alter the content of the consensus while keeping the Washington bit intact. For the World Bank and IMF still have a shopping list of appropriate policies for emerging economies.

But it is worth looking at the lessons drawn from the crisis given that the original Washington Consensus did generate such spectacular growth in the countries that embraced it. A recent World Bank report concludes that the mistake was to overlook the importance of the institutional structure of economies.[9] The sound macroeconomic policies were applied regardless of the historical and cultural content of individual economies, as if there really were such as thing as a pure free market. Of course there is not, and it seems mad that anybody could have imagined otherwise. But it is not that obvious, except with hindsight, that there is any link between the need for a small government budget deficit and, say, the regulation of the banking system or the types of contract on which civil servants are employed.

There are empirical links between certain types of institutions in developing economies and their growth rates and poverty levels. Respect for property rights, honest civil servants and politicians, protection of investors' and depositors' rights, and so on, are all correlated with higher GDP and lower poverty and inequality. There is a similar link with strong shareholder rights, such as allowing small shareholders to vote by proxy, not setting too high a threshold for the calling of exceptional shareholder meetings, and making it possible for shareholders to oust directors. So in this sense the commonplace conclusion that, broadly speaking, 'crony capitalism' was to blame for the severity of the South East Asian crisis is vindicated.

This does not just mean the tendency of eminent politicians to appoint members of their family and entourage to all the top jobs. It includes, also, things like legal protections for creditors. For example, countries can be ranked according to whether or not their laws guarantee that secured creditors get paid first, whether there is an automatic stay on assets, whether managers are forced to leave a bankrupt company, and so on. The developed economies mostly enjoy a high score. So do many countries whose legal system is derived from the Anglo-Saxon tradition, including Hong Kong, Singapore and Thailand. But those with traditions more like the French or German – most of Latin America, South Korea and Japan – have a lower average score. The same groups do worse on indicators of accounting standards too.

This comparison prompts the interesting thought that if this is what constitutes crony capitalism, it is an ailment that ought not just to afflict developing countries. For Germany, too, has close links between banks and corporations not mediated by markets, overlaps of personnel and misty accounting standards. Even taking a narrower view of crony capitalism, the rich countries share with the developing countries many institutional problems. Russia is not alone in being plagued by the web of Mafia control ensnaring its businesses or by massive tax evasion; but Italy is a very wealthy country and Russia is not. The entire European Commission was forced to step down over allegations of fraud and mismanagement; the EU budget forms one of the world's biggest gravy trains. The Anglo-Saxons do not escape; after all, the US has given us the phrase 'pork barrel' politics.

Perhaps it is true, then, that in the end the rich are just different from the rest in having more money. The lesson seems to be that developing economies have to get their macroeconomic policies right (the first version of the

Washington Consensus); then their microeconomic policies and institutions right (the updated version). And then
they need to get richer too, because that is what really
helps weather the storms of financial crisis.

But I think this would be too defeatist a conclusion.
Just as the 1980s debt crisis spurred the afflicted countries
to cut deficits, liberalise their trade rules and start privatisation programmes, the 1990s crisis will set in train a
process of detailed institutional reform. The developed
economies should be busy applying the same logic to
themselves as well as hectoring poorer countries about
what they ought to do. As indeed they are. Long
depression has forced institutional change on Japan, and
persistently high unemployment and low growth are seem-
ingly starting to do the same in Germany and France.
More equal access to education and health care in the US
might give young men in its ghettos an alternative career
to prison. There cannot be one Washington Consensus
for the poor and another for the rich.

Reform of the IMF and the World Bank

That leaves the question of the future of the two key
formal institutions of global economic governance, the
Bretton Woods sisters in Washington. The immediate
aftermath of crisis brought many proposals for sweeping
new institutional arrangements. George Soros proposed a
new authority to insure investors against debt defaults,
and others suggested an international bankruptcy court
or global financial regulator. But all fell by the wayside,
for several reasons. One was lack of political appetite for
yet more big international bureaucracies when it was not
clear that the many we already had were working.
Another was the degree of practical difficulties involved.

How could an international bankruptcy treaty incorporate extremely varied traditions in commercial law? How would a deposit insurance authority set limits on how much banks could loan or decide what premiums to charge? A further reason was that it was not obvious that the proposed institutions actually would prevent crises or change the pressures for the G7 and the IMF to get involved in crisis management.

A different type of proposal is the suggestion either for a new world monetary authority or for the IMF to preside over a return to fixed exchange rates as a prelude to a global currency. The idea harks back to the original Bretton Woods system set up after the Second World War. It broke up essentially because of inflationary policies which the US was unwilling to correct during the era of the Vietnam War. At the time the new neo-liberal intellectual trend also made a powerful case for a switch to floating exchange rates. The pendulum has certainly swung back now. The IMF has warned small economies against any middle-way exchange rate policy: either they must fix the currency or be prepared to let it float freely. The experience of countries like Thailand showed that setting a rate without a full and credible commitment to preserve it (including a high level of foreign currency reserves) could be extremely damaging. A growing number of smaller countries are opting to fix their rates, either through dollarisation or currency boards in Latin America or applying to join the euro in Central and Eastern Europe.

Robert Mundell, the 1999 Nobel Prize-winner in economics, is an ardent advocate of moving towards a global currency. He argues that if all major central banks accept the desirability of keeping inflation low and stable, and if all are targeting a common global price index, a permanently fixed set of exchange rates would be feasible. He describes massive fluctuations between currencies as 'dysfunctional'.[10]

The proposal was discussed by the G7 in 1987 but was derailed by that year's stockmarket crash. Besides, it is hard to see a realistic chance of the US at present conceding the need to replace the dollar with a global currency. The IMF also remains intellectually committed to freely floating exchange rates. Perhaps if the euro becomes increasingly important and the yen's status recovers with the Japanese economy, the political feasibility will improve. The technical feasibility has been hugely enhanced by the fact that the international financial markets are now entirely electronic. The stream of zeros and ones can easily be denominated in any units. And it is hard to disagree with Mundell's view that there is no good reason for an exchange rate to swing by 30 per cent or 50 per cent in a year, as they now can do.

More immediate issues facing the IMF are its role in crisis management and its status as an international 'lender of last resort'. Again, the crisis brought proposals for it to take on both these roles. But in practice it already does. The Fund acted as the executive arm of the G7, especially the US Treasury, in responding to the recent crisis. It has since started a process of scrutinising its own effectiveness and is, indeed, learning by experience.

As for serving as the body that steps in with funds during a crisis, it also did this to a degree. The question here is whether the amount of finance available to the IMF should be increased. It has roughly $200bn available to lend, or less than a fifth of the resources it had when it was first created, measured as a share of world GDP. Should its pool of funds therefore be increased to around $1 trillion? Even if its shareholders – the member countries – would provide the additional money, there is a good argument against it. That is the 'moral hazard' case. Knowing that the IMF had massive rescue funds available would encourage banks to make risky loans, and would encourage national regulators to relax, at a time when exactly the opposite is needed. In practice it has turned out to have adequate funds for the various rescue packages. The IMF or G7 were never about to run out of money to bring the crises to an end.

There is an active debate about whether the Fund should restrict itself to monetary and financial management and crisis resolution, leaving to the World Bank the long-term development programmes it has increasingly operated. The World Bank has very successfully redefined itself as an institution focused on poverty reduction and economic and social development. So it would be natural for the IMF to focus on complementary rather than competing roles. However, the IMF management and some G7 countries have so far resisted this US-inspired suggestion.

The key issue for both institutions in future must be an admission that they play an inescapable political role. Neither is a disengaged technocracy. Both must improve their own openness and transparency, and both must become more accountable to the poor countries which form their main clientele. Although countries are obviously unequal in power, globalisation must deliver benefits to the poor as well as the already-rich, and the international financial institutions will be despised and irrelevant if they do not make themselves accountable to all their members.

The French government proposed, in 1999, an explicit political role for the so-called 'Interim Committee' (later 'International Monetary and Financial Committee') of the IMF, its management board. The US blocked the plan, though compromising by accepting Gordon Brown, the UK chancellor and a heavy-hitting political figure, as its chairman. However, the US remained resistant to the idea of explicitly politicising the IMF and World Bank. One early sign of the resulting diplomatic tensions was the delay in finding a widely acceptable candidate to replace Michel Camdessus as head of the IMF when he retired in early 2000.

Conclusion

The global financial crisis of 1997–8 revealed the vulnerability of the emerging market nations and developed economies alike to the forces of globalisation. It highlighted the need for the governance of the world economy to catch up with the pace and degree of integration through trade and financial markets. This book has argued passionately in favour of the benefits of free markets, despite the crisis. Not only is the freedom to exchange and invest valuable in itself, like other freedoms, but it is also the only sure route to economic development. Further liberalisation of trade and investment, appropriately regulated, is essential if developing countries are to attain higher living standards. Economic growth in turn will slow population growth and create a constituency for environmental action in the developing world. However, there is certainly a powerful case for a reassessment of the role and capabilities of the international financial institutions. These need to be able to reflect a more even balance of power despite the dominance of the US in today's world economy. They also need to live up to their own rhetoric of transparency and accountability. The political economy of international governance is shifting substantially, with information technology enabling the development of a global opposition to the inter-governmental organisations. Campaigners acclaim it as more democratic than international bureaucracies, but Internet radicalism is not obviously accountable and responsive itself.

There is a rare opportunity, in the aftermath of a severe financial crisis and at a time of unusual economic potential, to harness the appetite for change in order to improve the governance of the world economy. Michel Camdessus said, in the speech earlier cited:

> We are the first generation in history to be called upon to organise and manage the world, not from a position of power such as Alexander's or Caesar's or the Allies' at the end of World War II, but through a recognition of the universal responsibilities of all peoples, of the equal right to sustainable development, and of a universal duty of solidarity.[11]

It would be a failure of historic proportions if the international community, both the formal powers and their informal opponents, missed this chance.

Notes

Introduction

1 George Soros, *The Crisis of Global Capitalism*, Little, Brown, 1998.
2 Paul Krugman, *The Return of Depression Economics*, Penguin, 2000.

Chapter 1   Frankenstein Finance

1 Frank Partnoy, *F.I.A.S.C.O.*, W.W. Norton, 1997.
2 Barry Eichengreen, *Globalizing Capital: A History of the International Monetary System*, Princeton University Press, 1996, p. 94.
3 See Francis Fukuyama, *The End of History and The Last Man*, Free Press/Hamish Hamilton, 1992.
4 Robert Skidelsky, Nigel Lawson, John Flemming, Meghnad Desai and Paul Davidson, *Capital Regulation: For and Against*, Social Market Foundation, February 1999, pp. 1–18.
5 Thomas Friedman, *The Lexus and the Olive Tree*, Harper-Collins, 1999, p. 308.
6 Martin Feldstein, 'Refocusing the IMF', *Foreign Affairs*, vol. 77, no. 2, March/April 1998, p. 61.
7 Friedman, *The Lexus*, p. 144.
8 Amartya Sen, *Development as Freedom*, Oxford University Press, 1999.

9   Dani Rodrik, *The New Global Economy and Developing Countries: Making Openness Work*, Overseas Development Council, Washington, 1999.

10   World Bank, *Beyond the Washington Consensus*, April 1999.

11   Interviews with OECD staff.

12   Paul Krugman, *The Return of Depression Economics*, Penguin, 2000.

13   Jeffrey Sachs, 'Global Capitalism', *The Economist*, 12 September 1998.

14   J.K. Galbraith, *The Great Crash, 1929*, first published 1954, Penguin, 1992.

15   Skidelsky et al., *Capital Regulation*, p. 43.

16   Manuel Castells, *The Information Age, Vols I–III*, Blackwell, 1994–6.

Chapter 2   Myths and Reality in Financial Markets

1   Richard Brealey, *The International Financial Architecture*, Bank of England policy paper, November 1998, p. 1.

2   Dani Rodrik, *The New Global Economy and Developing Countries: Making Openness Work*, Overseas Development Council, Washington, 1999.

3   Barry Eichengreen, 'Taming Capital Flows'. <http://emlab.berkeley.edn / users / eichengr / worlddevelopment2.pdf>.

4   Adrian Wood, *North–South Trade, Employment and Inequality*, Oxford University Press, 1995, pp. 191–212.

5   Paul Volcker, *Emerging Economies in a Sea of Global Finance*, Charles Rostov Lecture, School of Advanced International Studies, Washington, April 1998. <http://www.sais-jhu.edu/pubs/speeches/voltxt.htm>.

6   Eichengreen, 'Taming Capital Flows'.

7   J.M. Keynes, *A Tract on Monetary Reform*, first published 1923, Royal Economic Society, Cambridge, 1971, p. xvii.

8   Amartya Sen, *Development as Freedom*, Oxford University Press, 1999, p. 126.

9 Danny Quah, *The Weightless Economy in Economic Develop-ment*, World Institute for Development Economics Research, Working Paper no. 155, January 1999.
10 David Landes, *The Wealth and Poverty of Nations*, Little, Brown, 1998, pp. 50–7.
11 Karl Polanyi, *The Great Transformation*, Beacon Press, 1944, p. 209.
12 J.K. Galbraith, *The Culture of Contentment*, Houghton Mif-flin, 1992.
13 John Gray, *False Dawn: The Delusions of Global Capitalism*, Granta, 1998.
14 Martin Jacques, 'The Death of Neo-Liberalism', *Marxism Today, Wrong!*, special issue, November/December 1998, p. 2.

Chapter 3   Division of the Spoils

1 Fred Bergsten, *The Global Trading System and the Developing Countries in 2000*. <http://www.iie.com/catalog/WP/1999/ 99–6.htm>.
2 Adrian Wood, *North–South Trade, Employment and Inequal-ity*, Oxford University Press, 1995.
3 Paul Krugman, *Pop Internationalism*, MIT Press, 1996, p. 38.
4 Benjamin R. Barber, *Jihad vs McWorld: How Globalism and Tribalism are Reshaping the World*, Ballantine Books, 1996.
5 Bergsten, *The Global Trading System*.
6 United Nations Development Programme, *Human Devel-opment Report*, 1999, p. 70.

Chapter 4   A New International
Architecture

1 Jeffrey Sachs, 'Global Capitalism', *The Economist*, 12 Sep-tember 1998.
2 International Monetary Fund, *IMF-Assisted Programs in*

Indonesia, Korea and Thailand: A Preliminary Assessment, IMF Occasional Paper no. 178, September 1999.

3   Paul Krugman, 'Saving Asia: It's Time to Get Radical', *Fortune,* 9 July 1998. <http://www.fortune.com/fortune/ investor/1998/980907/sol.html>.

4   Paul Krugman, *The Return of Depression Economics,* Penguin, 2000, p. 146.

5   Lawrence Summers, 'Roots of the Asian Crises and the Road to a Stronger Financial System', speech at the Institute of International Finance, 25 April 1999. <http:// www.ustreas.gov/press/releases/pr3102.htm>.

6   John Eatwell, *International Capital Markets and the Future of Economic Policy,* working paper, 1998.

7   George Soros, *The Crisis of Global Capitalism,* Little, Brown, 1998.

8   Allan H. Meltzer (ed.), *Report of the International Financial Institution Advisory Commission.* <http://phantom-x.gsia. cmsu.edu/IFIAC/>.

9   Andrew Marr, *Ruling Britannia,* Michael Joseph, 1995.

10 United Nations Development Programme, *Human Development Report,* 1999, pp. 100–1.

Chapter 5   The New 'New Economy'

1   David Roche, 'The "Global" World is Anglo-Saxon', *Wall Street Journal Europe,* 5 January 2000.

2   Bruce Shapiro, 'The Seeds of Seattle'. <http://www. salonmagazine.com/news/feature/1999/12/08/wto/>.

3   Doreen Massey, 'Power Geometries and the Politics of Space-Time', Hettner Lecture, British Sociological Association, 1998, reprinted in Avtar Brah, Mary Hickman and Máirtín Mac an Ghaill (eds), *Future Worlds: Migration, Environment and Globalization,* Macmillan, 1999, pp. 13, 17.

4   Ibid., p. 17.

5   Paul David, 'The Dynamo and the Computer: An Historical Perspective on Productivity Paradox', *American Economic Review Papers and Proceedings,* no. 80, 1990.

6   Thomas Carothers, 'Think Again: Civil Society', *Foreign Policy*, Winter 1999–2000. <http://www.columbia.edu/~jb38/papers.htm>.

7   Michel Camdessus, 'From the Crises of the 1990s to the New Millennium', speech, 27 November 1999. <http://www.imf.org/>.

8   Amartya Sen, *Development as Freedom*, Oxford University Press, 1999.

9   World Bank, *Beyond the Washington Consensus*, April 1999.

10 Interview, *The Independent*, 17 January 2000.

11 Camdessus, 'From the Crises of the 1990s'.

Bibliography

Many relevant official communiqués, working papers and newspaper articles can be accessed through the Asia Crisis homepage run by Nouriel Roubini: <http://www.stern.nyu.edu/~nroubini/AsiaHomepage.html>.

Alesina, Alberto, 'The Political Economy of Macroeconomic Stabilizations and Income Inequality: Myths and Reality', in Vito Tanzi and Ke-young Chi (eds), *Income Distribution and High-Quality Growth*, MIT Press, 1998.

Barber, Benjamin R., *Jihad vs McWorld: How Globalism and Tribalism are Reshaping the World*, Ballantine Books, 1996.

Barro, Robert, *Determinants of Economic Growth: A Cross-Country Empirical Study*, MIT Press, 1997.

Bauman, Zygmunt, *Globalization: The Human Consequences*, Cambridge: Polity, 1998.

Bergsten, Fred, *The Global Trading System and the Developing Countries in 2000.* <http://www.iie.com/catalog/WP/1999/99-6.htm>.

Bhagwati, Jagdish, 'Why Free Capital Mobility May Be Hazardous to Your Health: Lessons from the Latest Financial Crisis'. <http://www.columbia.edu/~jb38/papers.htm>.

Brealey, Richard, *The International Financial Architecture*, Bank of England policy paper, November 1998.

Cable, Vincent, *Globalisation and Global Governance*, Royal Institute for International Affairs, 1999.

Calomiris, Charles, 'Blueprints for a New Global Financial Architecture', working paper, October 1998.

Camdessus, Michel, 'From the Crises of the 1990s to the New Millennium', speech, 27 November 1999. <http://www.imf.org>.

Carothers, Thomas, 'Think Again: Civil Society', *Foreign Policy*, Winter 1999–2000. <http://www.foreignpolicy.com/articles/winter1999-2000/thinkagain/carothers.html>.

Castells, Manuel, *The Information Age, Vols I–III*, Blackwell, 1994–6.

Coyle, Diane, *The Weightless World*, Capstone, 1997.

David, Paul, 'The Dynamo and the Computer: An Historical Perspective on the Productivity Paradox', *American Economic Review Papers and Proceedings*, no. 80, 1990.

Eatwell, John, *International Capital Markets and the Future of Economic Policy*, working paper, 1998.

Eatwell, John and Taylor, Lance, *Global Finance at Risk: The Case for International Regulation*, New Press, 1999.

Eichengreen, Barry, *Globalizing Capital: A History of the International Monetary System*, Princeton University Press, 1996.

Eichengreen, Barry, *The Only Game in Town*, working paper, November 1998.

Eichengreen, Barry, 'Taming Capital Flows'. <http://www.emlab.berkeley.edm/users/eichengr/worlddevelopment2.pdf>.

Evans, Huw, 'Debt Relief for the Poorest Countries: Why Did It Take So Long?', *Development Policy Review*, vol. 17, no. 3, September 1999.

Feldstein, Martin, 'Refocusing the IMF', *Foreign Affairs*, vol. 77, no. 2, March/April 1998.

Friedman, Thomas, *The Lexus and the Olive Tree*, Harper-Collins, 1999.

Fukuyama, Francis, *The End of History and The Last Man*, Free Press/Hamish Hamilton, 1992.

G22 Report, *Report of the Working Group on International Financial Crises, on Transparency and Accountability, on Strengthening Financial Systems*, Washington, October 1998.

Galbraith, J.K., *The Culture of Contentment*, Houghton Mifflin, 1992.

Galbraith, J.K., *The Great Crash, 1929*, first published 1954, Penguin, 1992.

Gray, John, *False Dawn: The Delusions of Global Capitalism*, Granta, 1998.

Held, David, McGrew, Anthony, Goldblatt, David and Perraton, Jonathan, *Global Transformations*, Polity, 1999.

Henderson, David, *The Changing Fortunes of Economic Liberalism*, Institute of Economic Affairs, London, 1998.

Hirst, Paul and Thomson, Graham, *Globalization in Question*, first published 1996, 2nd edn, Polity, 1999.

Huntington, Samuel, *The Clash of Civilizations and the Remaking of World Order*, Simon & Schuster, 1996.

International Monetary Fund, *IMF-Supported Programs in Indonesia, Korea and Thailand: A Preliminary Assessment*, IMF Occasional Paper no. 178, September 1999.

International Monetary Fund, *Progress in Strengthening the Architecture of the International Monetary System*, IMF Interim Committee, April 1999.

International Monetary Fund, *World Economic Outlook*, April 1998, October 1998, April 1999. <http://www.imf.org>.

Kelly, Kevin, *New Rules for the New Economy*, Fourth Estate, 1998.

Keynes, J.M., *A Tract on Monetary Reform*, first published 1923, Royal Economic Society, Cambridge, 1971.

Kindelberger, Charles, *Manias, Panics and Crashes*, first published 1978, 3rd edn, John Wiley, 1996.

Krueger, Ann, 'Whither the World Bank and IMF?', *Journal of Economic Literature*, vol. XXXVI, no. 4, December 1998.

Krugman, Paul, 'The Eternal Triangle'. <http://web.mit.edu/krugman/www/triangle/html>.

Krugman, Paul, *Pop Internationalism*, MIT Press, 1996.

Krugman, Paul, *The Return of Depression Economics*, Penguin, 2000.

Krugman, Paul, 'Saving Asia: It's Time to Get Radical', *Fortune*, 9 July 1998. <http://www.fortune.com/fortune/investor/1998/980907/sol.html>.

Lal, Deepak, *Unintended Consequences*, MIT Press, 1999.

Landes, David, *The Wealth and Poverty of Nations*, Little, Brown, 1998.

Lapham, Lewis, *The Agony of Mammon*, Verso, 1999.

Luttwak, Edward, *Turbo-Capitalism*, Weidenfeld & Nicolson, 1998.

Marr, Andrew, *Ruling Britannia*, Michael Joseph, 1995.

Marxism Today, *Wrong!*, special issue, November/December 1998.

Massey, Doreen, 'Power Geometries and the Politics of Space-Time', Hettner Lecture, British Sociological Association, 1998. Reprinted in Avtar Brah, Mary Hickman and Máirtín Mac an Ghaill (eds), *Future Worlds: Migration, Environment and Globalization*, Macmillan, 1999.

Meltzer, Allan H. (ed.), *Report of the International Financial Institution Advisory Commission*. <http://phantom-x.gsia.cmsu.edu/IFIAC/>.

Olsen, Mancur, 'Big Bills Left on the Sidewalk: Why Some Countries Are Rich and Others Poor', *Journal of Economic Perspectives*, Spring 1996.

Oxford Review of Economic Policy, *The Twentieth Century*, special issue, vol. 15, no. 4, Winter 1999.

Partnoy, Frank, *F.I.A.S.C.O.*, W.W. Norton, 1997.

Polanyi, Karl, *The Great Transformation*, Beacon Press, 1994.

Proudman, James and Redding, Stephen, *Openness and Growth*, Bank of England, 1998.

Quah, Danny, *The Weightless Economy in Economic Development*, World Institute for Development Economics Research, Working Paper no. 155, January 1999.

Roche, David, 'The "Global" World is Anglo-Saxon', *Wall Street Journal Europe*, 5 January 2000.

Rodrik, Dani, *The New Global Economy and Developing Countries: Making Openness Work*, Overseas Development Council, Washington, 1999.

Rogoff, Kenneth, 'International Institutions for Reducing Global Financial Instability', *Journal of Economic Perspectives*, Fall 1999.

Rossi, Marco, *Financial Fragility and Economic Performance in Developing Countries: Do Capital Controls, Prudential Regulation and Supervision Matter?*, International Monetary Fund Working Paper 99/66, 1 May 1999.

Sachs, Jeffrey, 'Global Capitalism', *The Economist*, 12 September 1998.

Sassen, Saskia, *Globalization and Its Discontents*, New Press, 1998.

Sen, Amartya, *Development as Freedom*, Oxford University Press, 1999.

Shapiro, Bruce, 'The Seeds of Seattle'. <http://www.salonmagazine.com/news/feature/1999/12/08/wto/>.

Skidelsky, Robert, Lawson, Nigel, Flemming, John, Desai, Meghnad and Davidson, Paul, *Capital Regulation: For and Against*, Social Market Foundation, February 1999.

Soros, George, *The Crisis of Global Capitalism*, Little, Brown, 1998.

Stopford, John, 'Think Again: Multinational Corporations', *Foreign Affairs*, Winter 1998–9.

Stopford, John and Strange, Susan, *Rival States, Rival Firms*, Cambridge University Press, 1999.

Summers, Lawrence, 'Roots of the Asian Crises and the Road to a Stronger Financial System', speech at the Institute of International Finance, 25 April 1999. <http://www.ustreas.gov/press/releases/pr3102.htm>.

United Nations Development Programme, *Human Development Report*, 1999.

Volcker, Paul, 'Emerging Economies in a Sea of Global Finance', Charles Rostov Lecture, School of Advanced International Studies, Washington, April 1998. <http://www.sais-jhu.edu/pubs/speeches/voltxt.htm>.

Wolf, Martin, 'Uncivil Society', *Financial Times*, 1 September 1999.

Wood, Adrian, *North–South Trade, Employment and Inequality*, Oxford University Press, 1995.

World Bank, *Beyond the Washington Consensus*, April 1999.

World Bank, *Global Economic Prospects and the Developing Countries: Beyond Financial Crisis*, September 1999.

World Bank, *World Development Report*, 1997, 1998, 1999. <http://www.worldbank.org/>.

Index